For Ralph Noble
a great educator
Ray Moley

9/10/42

THE
REPUBLICAN
OPPORTUNITY

Early in 1961 Raymond Moley determined to have a long, hard look at the house of America—its two-hundred-year-old foundations, the structure built thereon in the past twenty-five years, and the blueprints for reconstruction prepared by the dominant architects in Washington. The result is this sharply concise book.

The author's tools are common sense, abundant information, and fifty years of experience in and around politics and government at all levels. He has outlined the specifications of a better destiny for our Federal republic—a more secure and hopeful future devoid of mythical, implausible political plans and irresponsible, profligate management.

For those who oppose the present course of national policies, Mr. Moley portrays the value of the two-party system, and, within that system, the Republican Party as a means for viable progress. But a party invigorated, strengthened, and designed to meet the need of a civilization old in time but vitally concerned with meeting new conditions and problems. A party equipped, as one individual who has read Mr. Moley's manuscript says, with a viable philosophy and also with the practical means of gaining the authority to lead the nation. Here is light on how we got where we are, where we should go, and how to get there.

Also by RAYMOND MOLEY

THE
REPUBLICAN
OPPORTUNITY

by

RAYMOND MOLEY

DUELL, SLOAN AND PEARCE

New York

First edition

Affiliate of
MEREDITH PRESS
Des Moines & New York

Library of Congress Catalogue Card Number: 62-15463

MANUFACTURED IN THE UNITED STATES OF AMERICA FOR MEREDITH PRESS

VAN REES PRESS   •   NEW YORK

To

FRANCES SLEEPER MOLEY

REPUBLICAN

Who Proves Her Party Faith
By Hard Work for the Candidates
Of Her Party

Acknowledgments

In a book with this wide range of subject matter the author has an obligation to countless individuals whose wisdom has influenced his selective judgment over the years. These must be unnamed, although they are not forgotten.

I have had the collaboration of my son, Raymond Moley, Jr., in the composition of the entire text.

I have also had the editorial assistance and advice of Marjorie Wilson, who over a period of twenty years has been my assistant in the writing of hundreds of magazine and newspaper articles and six books.

Robert Humphreys, formerly campaign manager of the Republican National Committee, read the entire manuscript and strengthened the text with innumerable wise suggestions.

Grateful acknowledgment is also made to Republican Chairman Ray C. Bliss of Ohio for hours of discussion concerning party organization.

Herbert Miller, consultant of the Tax Foundation, and René Wormser have strengthened certain chapters by critical comments and advice. Emily Hammond, as I have indicated in the text, gathered the statistical and factual information upon which the welfare chapters are based. Harry Homewood contributed helpfully to the treatment of the farm problem. On monetary policy I have used a statement prepared for me by Ralph Robey.

The sympathetic interest of the publishers in the purpose and nature of the book has been a major source of encouragement.

I add also the routine acceptance of responsibility for such errors and shortcomings as have been unavoidable.

RAYMOND MOLEY

New York
June, 1962

Contents

THE CONSERVATIVE PROTEST

THE REPUBLICAN ALTERNATIVE

PRINCIPLES AND POLICIES— A PERSONAL APPRAISAL

CONCLUSION

The Genesis, Nature, and Purpose of This Book

ANYONE who ventures to offer an addition to the flood of recent literature on public affairs has a duty to prove necessity—or at least desirability. He should ask himself certain questions and reply to them.

Why write this book?

In the past twenty-nine years I have had a rather unusual opportunity to present my views of politics, government, and related affairs to the public under my name. God willing, I shall make use of that opportunity for some years to come. In that time I have written more than 1,500 weekly magazine articles and 3,150 newspaper columns. That sum of 4,650 would seem to have covered the subject fairly well. But many of those contributions are, so far as the specific subjects covered are concerned, dated now by ever-changing circumstances. However, throughout those "brief chronicles of the time" there have been woven certain consistent principles which, I believe, have important bearing on the choices which face the American people now in the 1960's. This book represents an effort to bring those principles and their application to the current scene in a way that is prohibited in the normal avenues of journalism.

Why write it now?

I shall not use such threadbare clichés as "time for greatness," "time for decision," or "time of crisis" to justify writing these comments at this time. Politics is a perpetual emergency. Decisions are not made at any specific moment once and for all in public affairs. Every year and every day new issues and decisions are presented to Congress, the Executive, and the public for decision. But each should be squared with the lessons of experience and reason and guided by unchanging basic patterns. Innumerable themes and variations are what enrich the piano compositions that have poured out over the decades and centuries, but the bars of black and white on the keyboard remain the same. The task of the composer is to fit his inspiration into the unity of his medium.

Two special circumstances in the current scene suggest the importance of applying permanent principles to the issues which in great variety fill the headlines these days. One is the presence of an Administration in Washington dedicated to what in current terminology is called liberalism. The slogans and political catchwords which this regime has used suggest that the nation must enter new areas of adventure and measurably change the course followed in the past.

In opposition to most of the new proposals there is a considerable but indeterminate body of protest that calls itself conservatism.

It is essential to remind those who call themselves conservative that they cannot meet successfully those innovations presented by liberalism with mere reiteration of basic principles, but only by examination of each issue in the context of alleged necessity. Also, that the direction of policy cannot be changed by mere opposition. And finally, that in our still intact system of popular government national policies must be changed by political action within the framework of our two-party system. Those three essentials I have endeavored to delineate in the chapters of this book.

Why a personal expression of opinion?

This is not a product of a committee, a convention, or of a parliamentary group. Manifestoes emanating from such collective efforts must and do express compromises, expediency, and selection. That is because of differences in emphasis, experience, and personal judgments from individual to individual. So far as the views presented herein are concerned, I have made only such compromises as seem to be compelled by my evaluation of the facts. Those views as set forth are the product of impressions and reflection over a long period during which I have been a witness to, and at times a participant in, the forming of national policies. In view of that, this book is written in the first person singular. But it is certainly not a memoir. Such autobiographical bits as appear here and there are included exclusively because they may underline the specific theme of the book.

The book, moreover, is presented to at least two generations, differing measurably in experience and outlook. In composing and editing the book I have had the collaboration of my son Raymond Moley, Jr., who entered the ranks of Harvard graduates after serving in the Second World War and who shares the advantages of a generation which is so actively examining the prospects in the years ahead and the bearing of present issues upon that future. The advantages of such a pooling of effort are obvious. Perhaps, except for the personal references and in the interest of simplicity, it might have been written in the first person plural.

Although since I reached voting age I have seen eight Presidents come and go and a ninth come to office, my contacts in teaching and otherwise during all that time have been with generations at the college age. I hope, therefore, I understand the emotional and intellectual reactions of the generation of the past decade.

Each of us draws his conclusions and shapes the emphasis of his opinions from a different personal position. For me or anyone to shape a philosophy or formulate a program that incorporates the innumerable shades of emphasis characterizing the views of all those who are opposed to current liberalism would fail miserably. I realize all too well that most liberals and a large number of conservatives will disagree with this book, in whole or in part. I have not sought to bend my views to fit the greatest possible number. To do so would destroy the integrity which my subject demands.

Why make it partisan?

This book is not a judicial evaluation of all sides of every issue it touches upon. It is a book of advocacy. It is an argument, not a mere recital or a stimulating intellectual exercise. It is partisan, but with the partisanship of conviction. Americans are not willing to submit their liberty to arbitration.

James Jackson Kilpatrick, an outspoken and notable journalist, uses an expression of opinion which I gratefully accept as representing my own position in this book:

With a few robust exceptions, our writers paint in pastels; our political scholars write a sort of ruffled-sleeve, harpsichord prose. We duel with soft pillows, or with buttoned foils; our ideas have lace on them. . . . These chamber music proprieties I acknowledge, simply to say, now, that the essay which follows should not be misunderstood. May it please the court, this is not a work of history; it is a book of advocacy. The intention is not primarily to inform, but to exhort. Its aim is not to be objective; it is to be partisan.[1]

My subject is not Kilpatrick's, although I adhere to his general thesis regarding states' rights. I am partisan first and foremost on ideological grounds. I reject as impractical and dangerous the philosophy and the bulk of the programs supported by those I call the liberals now established in power in Washington, in many academic chairs, and in a large part of the press and other media

[1] *The Sovereign States* (Chicago: Henry Regnery Company, 1957), p. ix.

of communication. By liberal Democracy I mean that group which is in control of the Democratic Party. I find ample agreement with many members of the minority of that party, in which Senator Byrd is such a luminous figure, as well as with a considerable number, perhaps a majority, of Republican members of both houses of Congress.

I am partisan, too, in a party sense. For it is my conviction that those who hold an ideological position measurably in common with my own must make themselves effective within the two-party tradition. Only by such a party allegiance and membership can the principles which we hold become national policy in the laws and executive actions of the republic. I have always rejected the concept that to rise above or slide below the party battle will ultimately change party policy. And there is not time, now that the liberals are gaining so rapidly, effectively to hide in the foxholes of critical detachment.

The Republican Party in the past quarter of a century has had a wealth of criticism from conservative quarters. But it has lost election after election because it has also had a poverty of workers. The Republican Party has many shortcomings which will be considered in this book. But those shortcomings can be corrected only as more individuals who oppose the liberal tide get into the Republican Party and work to elect its candidates, strengthen its organization, and rationalize its policies.

Why limit this book to domestic affairs?

The answer to this question is that there are virtues in brevity and inherent consistency. My son and I are not unaware of the grave international perils faced by this country and their impact on domestic affairs. We recognize the nature and malignant threat of Communism, its practice and pronouncements. We have both written on these subjects. The younger of us served in two wars, in one of which the United States was an ally of the Soviet Union and in the other fighting against Communist China and North Korea.

But conservatives have no monopoly on opposition to Communism. Conservatives and liberals alike have expressed their unalterable hostility to it. It would be a mistake to extend this book to encompass both domestic and international policies.

The safety of the nation from foreign enemies depends entirely upon its acceptance of domestic policies which make it strong and stable at home. Those policies are a major concern of this book.

Why limit consideration to Federal issues?

Here again the short answer will serve. The major issue before the nation is the extent to which the Federal government's powers and size impair the liberties of its citizens and destroy the integrity of the state and local communities. There are grave problems in state and local governments. But their consideration must wait for another occasion.

Expediency?

My concern here is not with what may be feasible in the light of present political conditions. I am not concerned with what is expedient and immediately possible of adoption. It is with what might be or ought to be in the future that certain sections of this book deal. Hence, in treating the problems of taxation, welfare, and other subjects, the reforms I suggest may have little chance of adoption in the immediate future. However, there are principles which must be in our minds and objectives to be kept in sight. It is not the length of the step. It is the direction. And the steps that will be taken by those vested with official authority in the future cannot be accurately anticipated.

About Words and Definitions

Certain words are not only means of quick identification but legal tender in the market place of ideas. I have used the terms "conservative" and "liberal" specifically in the context of their use in the United States in the mid-twentieth century. I use the terms "liberal" and "liberalism" as they provide identification now and in the United States for the dominant majority of the Democratic Party and its program. Moreover, I cannot concede the term "conservative" to individuals and groups whose overriding concern is anti-Communism. However, in the use of the word "conservative" to describe adherence to basic constitutionalism in domestic politics, the word serves to identify a general point of view.

The inadequacy of the terms "liberal" and "conservative" is shown by a tendency to qualify them with adjectival devices. A variety of such hyphenated qualifications has sometimes reached the absurdity of progressive- or liberal- or moderate- or dynamic-conservative. The Conservative Party in Canada is now called Progressive Conservative. Also, the Canadian Liberal Party has only a slight resemblance, so far as policies are concerned, to our liberal Democrats.

Those who are interested in the historical use of these words will find an illuminating discussion of the subject in a chapter in F. A. Hayek's fine essay, *The Constitution of Liberty,* called "Why I Am Not a Conservative." He rejects identification as a "conservative" because the use of the term in the Continental countries reaches such extremes as championship of a return to monarchy, and because in the Britain of the eighteenth century of Burke and the Pitts the Conservatives were favorable to a restoration of the royal prerogatives. Burke was neither liberal nor conservative. He was an Old Whig, and his ideological counterpart in the United States was James Madison. Hayek believes that the term "liberal" came into use through Adam Smith, who used it in an economic sense relating to support of the free market. In the first half of the nineteenth century in Britain liberalism was identified with such philosophers as John Stuart Mill and such statesmen as Cobden and Bright. Later it became the name of the

Liberal Party, which progressively moved toward greater and greater intervention and reached its summit in the social reforms of Lloyd George.

In its present American context I would define liberalism as support of greater Federal power, more intervention by government in economic life, greatly expanded welfare programs, and general hospitality to experiments and change of all sorts. The American conservative seeks more decentralization, the lessening of government intervention in personal and economic life, and adherence to the traditional principles of the Constitution. Both conservatism and liberalism at the moment are grievously embarrassed by their extremists. Among those who call themselves liberal there are many who would substantially transform the nation into a socialist-labor state. Among conservatives there are some who would use totalitarian methods to mobilize their attack upon liberalism.

An Inclusive Footnote

In 1952 I wrote and Alfred A. Knopf published a book entitled *How to Keep Our Liberty*. It was a summation of my views upon the national issues which confronted Americans in that year. This present book is in no sense a revision of that earlier volume. In a very few chapters, however, I have found certain language useful now, ten years later. In chapters 4, 24, 33, and 34 I have borrowed from myself without quotation marks, since I own the copyright and have the consent of the publisher to do so.

THE PRINCIPLES WE LIVE BY

CHAPTER 1

Faith and Good Works

SIXTY centuries of failure in men's striving for liberty under stable government look down upon our century and upon our institutions. They testify that men have not been capable of that self-discipline, fortitude, and strength essential to self-government for a long period. Many years of observation, experience, and reflection upon politics leave me with the conviction that our belief in the stability and permanence of free institutions is founded upon little demonstrable historical evidence.

Some years ago I devised a simple way to offer a perspective of the sweep of civilized time.

Suppose we think of history as a span of twelve hours. And that we are at high noon.

Last midnight, sixty centuries ago, the first traces of civilization emerged from the murk of savagery.

Then through the long hours of morning, man was a mere pawn in war and a unit of labor.

At dawn a Roman republic appeared and Pericles presided over an enlightened Athens. But within the hour, the Greeks were slaves and an emperor appeared in Rome who claimed he was God and by a combination of military force, public bribery through bread and circuses, and superstition implanted an imperial standard that was to remain for centuries.

3

At eight this morning Christ was born, taught the dignity of man, and was crucified.

As the sun rose higher Anglo-Saxon institutions slowly took form in the common law. This law was the creation of countless and unnamed individuals. It served as men's sole guard against arbitrary authority.

At twenty minutes after ten King John signed the Magna Charta, and a few minutes later Simon de Montfort and Edward I created a partially representative body, the English Parliament.

But four centuries passed before Englishmen exacted the Petition of Right from Charles I.

Forty minutes ago, after the Glorious Revolution, their basic liberties were reaffirmed in the English Bill of Rights.

Thirty minutes ago, at half past eleven, the United States, "conceived in liberty," appeared. Seconds later a lurid gleam of liberty flared in France and immediately died of its own excesses.

In the minutes since, in our own time, we have seen great nations try republican government and fall before dictators.

Here we are at high noon.

Where shall we be at five minutes after twelve? Who are we to think that our own freedom can stand against the grim evidence of the past?

We have nothing but our faith and the strength that springs from it. The proof eludes us. The evidence mocks us. Men's folly, their greed, and their mutual jealousies and hatreds have corroded free institutions over and over. These weaknesses are so obvious, human passions so easily stirred, that ambitious leaders, shrewd and unscrupulous, have used them from the beginning of time to subvert even the most rationally conceived systems of government.

And so our free institutions and individual liberty are founded upon faith—a fragile thing—and upon other essential virtues, hard-won and ever requiring renewal.

"The only faith," James Russell Lowell said, "that wears well and holds its color in all weathers, is that which is woven of conviction and sct with the sharp mordant of experience." Lowell's choice of "mordant" is apt and instructive. The word means a keen and caustic appraisal of realities. Lowell's inclusion of the words "in all weathers" also has significance. Our individual or personal faith ebbs and flows like the tide, from time of day to time of day. When we are tired or ill or frustrated, our faith will ebb. It revives with the morning, or with returning health or success. It ebbs when we are dismayed by failure or disaster at home and abroad. It flows again with better news.

Faith, however it may sustain our spirits and silence our doubts, is not enough. For mere faith may induce sufferance. In the context of this book, faith must find a partner in action. In religion, there have been those who held that faith alone is the way to salvation, and also those who stood for faith with good works. But in political life, faith without good works must perish.

The faculties of the mind must be sharpened to bring understanding of the perils that we face, the nature of our adversaries, and the character of their appeal to human beings altogether too receptive to illusions. We must equip ourselves with the means to match those adversaries.

Mere negation cannot suffice. Opposition and criticism are not enough even when, as now, the tide seems so surely to be running against us. The conservative must provide alternatives more appealing because they are more true. Indignation is no substitute for imagination.

Nor can there be any simple alternative. It is absurd simply to believe that all will be well if we rid ourselves of Communism at home and abroad, or that the way to sound government is to abolish the income tax, or that to re-establish the gold standard or to balance the budget alone will suffice. Americans are a long, long way from home. Liberalism has led us far afield. A comprehensive series of steps must be offered and vigorously exploited.

CHAPTER 2

The Paramount Individual

Our tradition of the supremacy of the individual over the state rests upon two vital factors. One was born of the acute physical compulsions of an exacting, severe life in a country all but destitute of civilization and law. The other came of an intellectual and moral renaissance in the native lands of those early American settlers, the roots of which are as old as the written history of mankind.

To rest our case for the paramount individual upon either of these factors at the expense of the other is to miss the significance of the institutions and principles we live by. Hardy, straight-backed self-reliance was nourished and disciplined in the hinterland of colonial and frontier America by the conditions imposed by an unsubdued natural environment. Individualism was an imperative of survival. Matters of artificial rank and privilege and the favor of distant authority mean little in such a situation. For primitive life creates its own leaders. He who can, by virtue of brain and brawn, face the perils of the wilderness and lead others to survival with him is recognized as the immediate source of decisions and strength. Faraway kings and governments have little means of making real the sovereignty they claim over areas recognizable to them only through the crude lines on roughly drawn maps. New forms of mutual living emerge under the rule of necessity.

But as Americans survived and prospered, their fortunate progeny was able to enjoy the riches of foreign culture. In the seventeenth and eighteenth centuries these heirs of pioneers were able to absorb the intellectual and moral values of Europe through whatever means of communication were available and through their travels. The Washingtons, Jeffersons, Madisons, and others were the heirs of earlier exponents of statecraft.

The intellectual life of Europe already had been quickened by a revival of ancient culture. Political life was drawing inspiration from a world's store of wisdom. The Enlightenment on the Continent taught the perfectibility of the individual. Constitutionalism in England taught how the worth of the individual might be made secure in the law of the land. Powerful religious tides accelerated the growth of liberty.

Concepts of individual liberty, upon which enlightenment and constitutionalism rested, were very old. Confucius, five centuries before Christ, taught that "Within the four seas all men are brothers." While he went from state to state in China seeking to build unity within the prevailing feudalism, there were several implicit and expressed truths. Among them was one which pointed out that the relation of brotherhood was imposed by the facts of nature. Another proclaimed that brotherhood meant equality. Mencius carried this concept further. Among his aphorisms are, "The sage emperors Yao and Shun are as ordinary people," and "All people can become Yaos and Shuns." Scattered through the teachings of the Hebrew prophets there is the same refrain of equality before God. In the vision of Micah it is said:

"For as all the peoples walk every one in the name of
    his God,
We will walk in the name of the Lord our God forever."

The Athenians under Pericles struggled for their ideals against neighbors who had chosen quite different concepts of the nature of the state. Pericles in his Funeral Oration professed most clearly the Athenian ideal. He underlined the fact that their political institutions rested upon the character of the people and that all individual freedom depended upon the education and wisdom of those who enjoyed that freedom.

Plato, born two years after the death of Pericles, faced the reaction which followed the wars between Athens and its rivals. In his long life he veered from a belief in individual freedom to the view that the right of the state should be supreme—a state ruled, incidentally, by philosopher kings.

We may conclude that Plato cared deeply for the individual. But he apparently came to believe that the values he so cherished could not be attained by the individual himself. They must be imposed by an elite. This comes close to present-day authoritarian forms of government. Essentially this view is held too by many Americans who seek the welfare of individuals through planning by an elite—the "we-elite."

The basic break by Aristotle from his teacher is reflected in his mature work, beginning after Plato's death in 347 B.C., when Aristotle was thirty-seven. In his *Nicomachean Ethics* Aristotle gives the name "happiness" to "the good we are seeking." The essence of his definition is that happiness is always "desirable in itself and never for something else." Thus, such values as money, property, pleasure, "reason and every virtue" are sought not for themselves but as a means to happiness. And since he recognized that the varying judgments of individuals would place different emphasis upon many means, there is implicit the concept of individual choice. This is quite unlike the Platonic concept of values imposed upon the individual by authority.

But equality in choice is only one element in the Aristotelian ethic. His ideal state would be a happy co-ordination of democracy, oligarchy, and executive authority within a constitutional order. It is true that Aristotle believed that some were "more equal than others," for he defended slavery and held the status of women in low esteem. But his enlightenment shone in the darkness of many centuries and had a firm place in shaping American principles.

It remained for a later age to incorporate, in constitutional and legal guarantees, individual rights, either general or specific— rights which might be enforced through the agency of the state. Undoubtedly, the most profound revolution in thought in the Western world concerning the basic importance of the individual came with the teachings of Christ and of the early Christians, notably St. Paul.

Without the contribution of Christian teaching, much of the laboriously reasoned egalitarianism taught by the Greeks and later by some Roman philosophers and lawmakers might have been lost. For neither by science, which could never hope to prove the basic equality of individuals, nor by rational conclusions, which would find little understanding in an age of illiteracy which prevailed for more than a thousand years, could the primacy of the individual hope to survive. But the simple concept of a brotherhood of all men, with a common destiny and a oneness with God, could become the bedrock on which later enlightenment could rest. Most important was the concept of the immortality of the soul. It became the major foundation of the individual's significance.

The intermittent appearances of the concept of free institutions have been mentioned in the preceding chapter. Here consider John Locke, who, as the "father of modern constitutionalism," profoundly contributed through Jefferson and others to the shaping of American political traditions.

Locke's *Two Treatises on Government* were not only a defense of the assertion of the sovereignty of the people in the revolution of 1688. They were a delineation of principles relevant to the creation of the United States as a nation and our own constitutional order. Locke, like Jefferson, held the natural law as the basis of individual rights. In so doing he followed the earlier exposition of the meaning of natural law by Hugo Grotius:

The law of nature is a dictate of right reason, which points out that an act, according as it is or is not in conformity with rational nature, has in it a quality of moral necessity; and that in consequence, such an act is either forbidden or enjoined by the author of nature, God.

The value of this concept is that, whether or not one wishes to ascribe natural law to the will of God, there is assigned a "right reason" which responds to the dictates of an inherent morality.

The individual's right to liberty is thus defined by Locke:

The liberty of man in society is to be under no other legislative power but that established by consent in the commonwealth . . . But freedom of men under government is to have a standard rule to live by, common to every one in that society, and made by the legislative power erected in it; a liberty to follow his own will in all things, where that rule prescribes not; and not to be subject to the inconstant, uncertain, unknown arbitrary will of another man: as freedom of nature is to be under no other restraint but the law of nature.

Of the right of property, Locke says:

The labor of his body and the work of his hands we may say are properly his. Whatsoever, then, he removes out of the state that nature hath provided and left it in, he hath mixed his labor with, and joined to it something that is his own, and thereby makes it his property. It being by him removed from the common state nature placed it in, it hath by this labor something annexed to it that excludes the common right of other men.

Jefferson in the Declaration of Independence, no doubt influenced by Aristotle, with whose writings he was quite familiar, substitutes "happiness" for "property." In the sense in which Aristotle used the word this was inclusive of property. The addition of the words "the pursuit of" means to me that happiness, or any of its components, is not to be imposed but to be subject to freedom of choice.

The Bill of Rights as well as other contemporary guarantees of individual freedom use Locke's trilogy—life, liberty, and property. Indeed, the entire structure of the American Bill of Rights, as well as the Constitution itself, constitutes an affirmation of the supremacy of the individual. The Constitution is "ordained and established" by "we the people." Rights not specifically delegated by the people through their representative bodies are retained by them. The citizen, moreover, is to be protected by and from the government he has authorized and from the majorities behind it. And, by the words of the Declaration of Independence, when their government no longer protects individual rights "it is the Right of the People to alter or to abolish it."

Thus was built into the American system of constitutional and legal order the principle that the individual is the master and the government his servant. This is what the United States presented to the world when the nineteenth century opened. At that time, too, the inauguration of the Jeffersonian Republican Party reinforced the individual's control of all governments by stressing the integrity of state and local authority.

While the new century was to witness a ruthless reexamination of many hitherto revered ideas concerning religion, human nature, and political authority, there was no loss of faith in man himself.

Professor Richard LaPiere, who deserves very high rank among contemporary social philosophers, stresses that durable tradition in *The Freudian Ethic,* where he points out that this nineteenth-century view of man "is in all salient purposes the exact antithesis to a view of man that has emerged during the present century and that seems well on the way toward becoming the prevailing ideal of the twentieth century." [1]

But, as John Stuart Mill commented a century ago:

To give any fair play to the nature of each, it is essential that different persons should be allowed to lead different lives. In pro-

[1] (New York: Duell, Sloan and Pearce, 1959), pp. 3–4.

portion as this latitude has been exercised in any age, has that age been noteworthy to posterity.

In the uneven flow of men's affairs the individual has always struggled for his identity. This is true even in the most despotic states of our time, while his voice may be smothered, his titles and estate confiscated, and his deviations ridiculed. He may be obliged to repudiate his opinions. But there is still his voice. Even while his knee is bent, his back may remain straight.

CHAPTER 3

The Individual's Community

THE BRITISH EMPIRE," said Gilbert K. Chesterton, "is like the passengers in an omnibus; there is unity only in an accident."

A collection of spectators watching a fire is not organized. Each individual is able to satisfy his curiosity as well, or better, if all others go away. But to do something about the fire organized effort is needed. The crowd becomes an association to fight the blaze and salvage property under some sort of direction. The individuals are at once united and concerned with each other.[1]

In the great flood in Dayton, Ohio, in 1913, city and state governments proved incompetent or unable to take effective measures to protect the city and its inhabitants. The president of the National Cash Register Company, esteemed and recognized as a leading citizen, organized the operation according to his own ideas and with his executive capacity. The wide respect in which he was held commanded the obedience of the citizenry. It mattered little to them that at the moment he was under Federal indictment by a distant government. He served a great and useful purpose and succeeded.

Some years earlier a tidal wave swept over the city of Galves-

---

[1] Robert M. McIver, *Community* (New York: The Macmillan Co., 1928), p. 25.

ton, Texas. There were leaders and there was community response.

Thus we see not only the action of community unity but of leadership as well. For in such instances the community creates its own leadership. There is a vitality of community as against legal authority created by legislative action at some remote capital. It is interesting that the communities of both Dayton and Galveston demanded and secured new forms of government. Later these forms became legal in countless communities over the nation.

In a crisis, when things need doing, our national statesmen turn to the community to effectuate efforts. In the fine-feathered sentiments of philosophers, politicians, and historians regarding the nation, the states, and the world, the word "community" is used only as it is torn from its traditional meaning and applied to those larger units of association. But the community, like a deep ocean stream, is the progenitor and still the vital substance for organized life.

In America, before there were colonies, there were communities. In the writing of the Constitution the community was unmentioned and unnoticed. But there it was—a foremost concern in the life, home, and hope of the individual—the cradle of his liberty.

The move toward centralization in the United States has been carried on under the screen of many familiar clichés. It has been characterized as an "inevitable drift." In our schoolrooms we are told that the development of means of communications and transportation, the growth of great enterprises dependent upon a national market, and the expansion of our consciousness from the "parochial" to national and world-wide concerns have made us "nationally oriented" and "world-minded." This jargon leads to the conclusion that the community is obsolete, its values quite out of date.

But in this country it was communities of individuals and their leaders that carried the battle to throw off British rule. Since the Revolution, however, the essential values of the community and its relation to individual liberty have been periodically swept under the rug and out of public notice. The movement that resulted in the formation and adoption of the Constitution was a reaction against the exercise of excessive power by states and the communities within them. Then in the long debate over slavery that preceded civil war the issue concerned the relations of the states and the Union. In the generation following the Civil War Americans undertook national expansion and development. They strode toward a "destiny." The agency that could best fulfill that destiny was an even more centralized government, supporting and accompanying large enterprises. The growth of railroads and industry became national in scope. Finally the "progressive movement" that began at the turn of the century and the liberalism of the years since 1933 drove a powerful tide toward greater and greater Federal centralism. Two world wars were important factors.

Still the local community is a tenacious entity and, despite the forces and influences ranged against it, a hardy institution, capable of stubborn resistance against its extinction. We need only to examine our political parties to see how communities have been recognized in these purely voluntary associations. The county, state, and national committees are representative bodies. Their basis is in the communities, whether these be urban wards and precincts or rural townships.

Moreover, waves of immigration brought a certain identity within communities based upon relationships in the Old World. Hence, all over the West and in the great Eastern cities individuals and families with common national origins clustered together. People do not leave their roots and associations behind. They transplant them in a new soil. Even within a nation we find this cohesion based upon common origins. For example, in the great modern county of Los Angeles we find communities largely composed of former residents of Iowa, or Illinois, or Kansas, or Texas.

Many who so vigorously promote Federal and now international authorities show their utter dependence upon the community and its innumerable sanctions and usefulness whenever they must impose really severe limitations upon individual freedom. Consider the exactions and controls imposed under the stress of the Second World War. In operating the draft it was necessary to set up local draft boards to make primary judgments as to which of many individuals should be called into the military service. In operating this coercive power no functionaries from Washington could have succeeded. Such power directly exercised would have been resisted and frustrated. It was instead delegated to a board of notable citizens of the community who were in a position to know at first hand the facts about eligibility. In imposing rationing local people were selected who would know who needed to use his automobile and for what purpose. Local groups controlled distribution of meat or sugar coupons.

But meanwhile in certain respects the growth of Federal power has had a dangerous effect upon community and individual life. The farming communities live under a vast Federal bureaucracy, with many, many farmers subsidized, Federal dependents. Liberals would impose their will upon the local communities in the vital area of public education, enforcing Federal standards and uniformity through Federal money.

Wherever individuals live close to one another co-operative relations form. If there is no law they create their own law. If there is no enforcement machinery they create something on the order of the old vigilance committees, execute their laws according to their own collective sense of what is right and wrong, and determine among themselves what punishments should be meted out to violators.

For years, because of the ceaseless influx of the foreign-born, especially in the great cities, the new immigrants found themselves in a strange country with a language alien to them and with no knowledge of the customs and laws for which respect was desirable. There arose, before government engaged in all manner of welfare, the "boss" and the "machine." The boss, sometimes of an earlier generation of immigrants, had learned "the ropes." His service to the new arrivals was most comprehensive. He cared for their needs, got them jobs, secured their citizenship, counseled them and their offspring, and won their dependence in a hundred ways. For this they gave him their political support. A sort of New World feudalism reigned in many big cities.

The New York City boss of bygone days was the best example. He held no public office, but he was the master of those who did. He made his own living by exploiting the city through available advantages of various sorts. These compensations were sometimes what "Boss" Plunkitt called honest graft—advantageous deals, frequently in real estate where public improvements were planned, sometimes in contracts with the city, and often in insurance and banking. Often, of course, the graft was illegal and reprehensible. But whatever his crudeness and his sins, the boss was a large factor in the community, often performing essential and wholesome services.

The welfare community provided by the boss's philanthropy has in recent years been supplanted by government welfare. The children of the early immigrants have grown up. Community life has been weakened. Therefore, like Othello, the boss's occupation is gone. In the 1961 Democratic primary election in New York City the loser, Tammany, was shattered perhaps beyond hope of revival by a curious "reform movement." The outcome of this cannot be predicted. Have we indeed in New York and elsewhere merely substituted the "incorruptible corruptor of all" for the older feudalism of the "machine"?

Within the community the attraction of a common interest pulls people together in still smaller associations for progress, promotion, and service. In them and in the local political parties there is source for hope.

But the damage is most vividly portrayed in the big cities. The community-inspired and -supported personal welfare programs have been supplanted by impersonal and often indiscriminate government welfare programs. Family and neighborly responsibilities have been undermined. The community in which there are ways of determining need has lost its discriminatory authority. In 1961 the city of Newburgh, New York, attempted to set up its own criteria of welfare. But immediately it was pounced upon by both state and Federal authority, armed with irresistible law.

Vast public housing developments and what is called "urban renewal," proposed and passed by Congress in the name of better living and more beautiful cities, have, often needlessly, uprooted old and well-integrated communities, scattering the inhabitants thereof throughout the cities. True, there are better roofs over their heads and, for the moment at least, cleaner surroundings. But these advantages are overmatched by the shattering of community reliability and sometimes family control. These Federal "gifts" take their toll in rootlessness and delinquency. The bureaucracy is not a good neighbor. It is not even a neighbor.

Like Goldsmith's deserted village, many communities are fading away. But it is not because wealth accumulates. It is because power accumulates, impersonal, inflexible, distant, cold.

CHAPTER 4

Our Entailed Inheritance

In the United States constitutional government serves two imperative purposes. Our Constitution provides a pattern within which men may live free and also gain for themselves that sufficiency of order essential to growth, progress, and internal peace. The body of the Constitution provides the latter; the Bill of Rights the former. It has been noted that the one is a Constitution of order; the other a Constitution of liberty.

Since, as Disraeli said a century ago, a nation lives only through its institutions, the colonies were compelled, when they broke the ties to England, to find a substitute for those institutions which cemented the British people as a nation. Those were the Crown, the Commons, and the Lords Temporal and Spiritual.

The foresight and experience of American statesmen counseled them to create a form of government suitable to citizens of a new civilization. They therefore took the great risk of committing the nation's destiny to a written instrument, an institution on paper, a compact among "the people of the United States and among the states already existing."

Throughout that written instrument there are clear evidences of the other purpose, which was dictated by a deep understanding of human character. For the Constitution is also a self-denying ordinance. This purpose is well described by Cornelia Le Boutellier:

19

Gregarious and social and political, loving to be free, man builds a state, the cornerstone of which is his inherent liking for his fellow man. Along with this inherent liking goes inherent faith, and a shrewd appraisal of his fellow man as a good sort, but a sort who "wants watching." So he sets up machinery for watching his fellow man through the ministrations of constitutional democracy and charges the state with the solemn duty both to keep him free and to hold him safe.[1]

The Americans who with force of arms tore themselves loose from Britain's rule were still the beneficial heirs of a great Anglo-Saxon tradition, the reign of law. This is what made possible their calculated rejection of monarchy. Bracton had said in 1250 that "Right is derived from what is unwritten and that which usage has approved." The individual's right over the centuries found a firm habitation in the common law. The state itself is the child of that law. The roots of that law elude even the onslaught of generations of historical probings. Edward Jenks in his *Law and Politics in the Middle Ages* says that law is

an authority which, for some reason or another, great masses of men feel themselves bound to follow, not because they choose, but because they must. And yet certainly it is not a command of the State, direct or indirect. Upon critical examination, it may turn out to be the work of a mere private composer. Why do men obey it? Further back again, we find a purely impersonal document, compiled, no one exactly knows how, or by whom; and yet it is the controlling force which shapes the daily conduct of men. . . . It is not the work of the State, it may not be recognized by the State, there may be no State to recognize it. Yet the essential ideas of Law, the evident ancestors of our modern juristic notions, are clearly there.[2]

Our constitutional system is only partially encompassed in what was written into the text of 1787 and in the subsequent Bill

---

[1] Cornelia Le Boutellier, *American Democracy and Natural Law* (New York: Columbia University Press, 1950), p. 55.
[2] (London: John Murray, 1898), pp. 2, 3.

of Rights. We observe in our law and custom a vastly greater inheritance. It has been likened to a great river of principle from which a small part was channeled by our statesmen into written form.

This is not the time or place to argue the case of "natural law." Suffice it to say that from Aristotle to Thomas Aquinas, to Grotius, to Burke and Jefferson the concept has successfully resisted the dialectic of lawgivers and lawyers. Whether it is embodied in the revealed word of God or whether it is an innate manifestation of the "right reason" of man, it has guided and at times supplied what is written or judicially expounded. A theory, perhaps, but one which has not only restrained and ordered the passing appetites and caprice of human beings but over the ages has been recognized and respected. It has made possible the reign of law and of governments restrained by law.

Implicit in the principle of the reign of law is consent of the governed. The majority governs. It does not rule. For under our Constitution there are clear implications that mere obedience is not the same as consent. Consent is not resignation, even to the inevitable. Consent is not agreement obtained by duress. Nor is it obtained by promises and propositions which under proof can be shown to be fraudulent or impossible of fulfillment.

My concept of consent as I formulated it in an earlier book is this: Consent is real when those involved freely, knowingly, willingly, and with a part in creating the situation involved, share the benefits and responsibilities of the decision.[3]

Like the recurrent theme of a great symphony, a concern for personal rights runs through the entire text and amendments of the Constitution. The Tenth Amendment suggests the anxiety of statesmen to linger on the subject and to encompass it in one sentence: "The powers not delegated to the United States by the Constitution, nor prohibited by it to the States, are reserved to the States respectively, or to the people."

[3] *How to Keep Our Liberty* (New York: Alfred A. Knopf, 1952).

The specified rights are those of "life, liberty, and property." These, it was assumed, were indivisible, equal, and interdependent.

The disposition of the United States Supreme Court to place property rights at a lesser level than life and liberty has encountered the sharp criticism of perceptive jurists. There can be no distinctions of value in appraising the trilogy of rights. They must stand or fall together.

The perils in a concentration of power were a primary concern of those who framed the Constitution. They well knew from reading past history and from their own experience the infection to which individuals vested with authority were so hospitable. Hence the division of powers among the three branches of government and the reservation of residuary power to the states and the people thereof.

Ambition [wrote Madison in *The Federalist*] must be made to counteract ambition. . . . It may be a reflection on human nature, that such devices should be necessary to control the abuses of government. But what is government itself but the greatest of all reflections on human nature? If men were angels, no government would be necessary. . . . In framing a government which is to be administered by men over men, the great difficulty lies in this: you must first enable the government to control the governed; and in the next place oblige it to control itself.

The size and great variety of the regional components of the nation which were apparent even in the eighteenth century are vastly emphasized in the twentieth. They argue decentralization of functions and authority of government. As we have learned in our experience as a nation, the logic of the Constitution is supported by emergent facts. Experimentation on a small area provides examples for all areas. That government serves best which is close to and under the scrutiny of the people. Jefferson made the observation that if the nation were not already divided into states, such a division would be necessary.

The foregoing principles embody our basic inheritance. Our

experience since their adoption has confirmed their validity. But with the passage of time we have enriched that inheritance with added principles.

The first of these to gain authority was the two-party system. An early fear that there might be a rise of innumerable factions created by conflicting interests was soon resolved by the emergence of two parties generally differing in their policies but sufficiently representative of the common concerns of all sections and states. Thus, they were able to provide alternative choices of policies and candidates for the electorate, to minimize abuses of power by mutual criticism, and to provide the frequent changes in control so essential to the invigoration of the body politic.

The parties, because of the vast area over which they were compelled to extend their organization, accommodated themselves to a multitude of divergent interests and to the nature of a classless society. There have been many who have noted the wide accommodation of party platforms and of the expressions of candidates to diverse interests and issues. This has been called hypocrisy, and generous helpings are frequently served up by party leaders as part of our political fare. But if ever there has been a value attained by generalities, it has been in our party system. It has prevented ills which have stricken and paralyzed assemblies, cabinets, and governments in other lands. Measurably, but not entirely, it has prevented the area of political discussion from being confused by the matters irrelevant to the process of government and the maintenance of constitutional rule—matters involving religious and racial prejudices, class divisions, and cults.

Slowly, over the years, basic differences have evolved which pertain to the fundamental character of the nation and its government. Today, they are resolving themselves into the broad issue of centralized versus decentralized government. This is an issue which is wholly relevant to the conflict of two parties.

Another stupendous achievement of the American people has been its maintenance over the generations of the ideal of a classless society. Somehow we have avoided the social and economic stratifications which have been the curse of older civilizations. Our good fortune in this respect has been in part due to our rapid economic growth, our capacity to expand opportunity for initiative and invention, and the flux in our society by successive waves of immigration. In this context of a society which rejects rigidity there is engendered optimism, high thinking, daring, and aggressiveness.

The foregoing principles come to us as a heritage not only validated by the wise counsel of our most illustrious ancestors, but proven in the test of years and of times of great trials and national peril. There is imposed upon us a sacred obligation which we cannot in honor reject—to preserve and pass on that heritage.

Edmund Burke reminded the British people in one of their most exacting hours:

You will observe that from Magna Charta to the Declaration of Right, it has been the uniform policy of our constitution to claim and assert our liberties, as an entailed inheritance derived to us from our forefathers, and to be transmitted to our posterity; as an estate specially belonging to the people of this kingdom, without any reference whatever to any other more general or prior right. . . . The idea of inheritance furnishes a sure principle of conservation, and a sure principle of transmission; without at all excluding a principle of improvement. It leaves acquisition free; but it secures what it acquires. . . . By a constitutional policy working after the pattern of nature, we receive, we hold, we transmit our government and our privileges. . . The institutions of policy, the goods of fortune, the gifts of Providence, are handed down to us, and from us, in the same course and order. . . . Thus, by preserving the method of nature in the conduct of the state, in what we improve we are not wholly new; in what we retain, we are not wholly obsolete. . . . In this choice of inheritance we have given to our frame of polity the image of a relation in blood.

It may profit all of us to heed these words. For they convey not just a nostalgic affinity to the past but a valid determination to foster the urge for improvement. We hold that wisdom of which we are the fortunate heirs. We must use that wisdom as the means for exploring and shaping an ever-enriched future. This is our inescapable obligation and responsibility.

CHAPTER 5

I Revisit the Constitution

IN this chapter, as elsewhere in this book, I shall, except when necessary, avoid reminiscence. Old soldiers never die. They still linger over the dinner table and fight forgotten battles with the deployment of knives, forks, and sugar bowls. Old politicians do not wither. They write memoirs.

I find it necessary here, however, to explain why I could not have written the preceding chapter when I was a student in college or graduate school, or as a professor of public law at Columbia. I knew the text of the Constitution and enough of its interpretation to teach it. I knew the words. But I never fully appreciated the intent of those who wrote it until I served at the higher level of the Federal government.

It is not without embarrassment that I recall that in the academic life in which I was a participant for a number of years before 1933 the Constitution of the United States and the tradition of which it was a part were the objects of biting criticism. The Constitution was written—so it was said, and so it was also written into textbooks—by men whose motives were solely to cement the power of the monied and commercial classes, to protect their own property interests, and even to feather their own nests. In the semantics of the time, the expression "founding fathers" was uttered with a sneer.

Young instructors assigned the *New Republic* as required

reading in their classes. The "brave new world" was with us, and the "copybook maxims" of which Kipling wrote in 1919 were anachronisms.

The law schools of the 1920's were taking up the new gospel, and the fundamentals of jurisprudence were set aside. Justice Holmes's "futilitarianism" spread to hundreds of young devotees. In the teaching of history and political science the role of "strong" Presidents was exalted. And the enlargement of Federal power became an obsession among the "intellectuals."

With what one historian called "the crisis of the old order" in the depression, reformers of all sorts rushed forth with blueprints for a new order. The inauguration of Franklin D. Roosevelt brought to Washington as miscellaneous a lot of individuals as had visited the capital since the famous inauguration of Andrew Jackson. The new group did not deface the White House furnishings as Jackson's backwoodsmen had done a century before. But they were quite willing to knock about the institutions of the republic.

No one who was not there in person can realize what an exciting, not to say terrifying, time it was. There were old socialists, municipal reformers, greenbackers, free silverites, public-ownership zealots, together with a large number of Wilsonian Democrats whose administrative skills had rusted during twelve years of Republicanism, and, as we learned later, a handful of Communists. They came in imposing numbers:

> "Singing songs of expectation,
> Marching to the Promised Land."

While room was made somehow for many of these, despite the poverty of competence which they represented, there were steadying influences for the first year or so. There were holdovers of experienced individuals, and there were a few sound Democrats like Jesse Jones and Lewis Douglas. The earlier reforms were salutary and necessary. The banks were saved and restored to solvency. The budget was drastically slashed. Herbert Hoover's Reconstruction Finance Corporation was extensively used.

In much of the other legislation which was demanded by the President and passed by an obedient Congress there were provisions which even their authors realized were probably beyond constitutional bounds. But they were adopted because of the emergency. The President was given immense discretionary authority. It was believed that the Supreme Court would care for matters of constitutionality in due time.

But by the time the Supreme Court had gotten around to making its decisions, the President had convinced himself that the measures were quite constitutional and that the Supreme Court was evil in its intentions, ignorant of the law, and usurping of authority. Hence the conflict began which ended in the President's plan for packing the Court.

My reflections, induced by what I saw in that first year and later, brought about a profound and lasting reappraisal of my earlier concepts of constitutional principles. In the first six months I was in the very eye of the hurricane. Later I was unofficially the President's helper in various tasks. This afforded me a close and intimate knowledge of the behavior of a man invested with great authority. I realized that I was talking with and observing a man whose hospitality for odd ideas of reform was almost without limit, whose enjoyment of the exercise of power was immense, and whose moods were unbelievably capricious. Fretting at the slow processes of legislative bodies, he had a habit of saying what he would do "when I get rid of Congress." I have already referred to the culmination of his wrath at the "nine old men" on the Supreme Court.

The bureaucracy proliferated. Intoxicated by the heady atmosphere, department and bureau heads were busy imposing upon the citizenry their own interpretations of the loose laws rushed through Congress. There was also growing evidence of that excessive tendency for intrigue and rivalry within the bureaucracy which has been a characteristic of government down the ages.

In the Congress itself, there was the tendency of politics to temper judgment. Concessions to pressure groups grew apace because of the overwhelming majority of the President's party and the weakness of the opposition. Traditional rights and responsibilities of the states and local governments were swept aside.

Measures of welfare originally dedicated to the temporary alleviation of poverty and need became fixed institutions of government and after the emergency passed were shamelessly used to snare votes and win the support of minority groups. The "general welfare" clause in the Constitution came to be the favorite tool for the welfare of the party in power.

Those years brought to me a comprehension of what wise men long ago were seeking through the limitations imposed by the Constitution. I was moved to reconstruct in my own mind what Hayek calls the "broken fragments of a tradition."

LIBERALISM'S SUPERSTATE

CHAPTER 6

The Anatomy of Liberalism

BEFORE seeking a definition of the strange superstructure which liberalism has been building upon the Doric simplicity of our constitutional system, it will be well to examine the mood, motives, and character of the liberals who have labored to create it. Unlike the archeologist, who must rummage among the bits and pieces that have survived the centuries, in this research we have a great advantage.

For the liberals are our contemporaries. We can observe their reactions, read and hear their words, and mark the catch of their breath as they face social and political problems. But there are several species of liberals. And these must be distinguished one from another.

There are those whose reasoning must be commended. They argue with a good deal of conviction that the individual's life becomes more and more complex as the population grows and human beings are huddled closer together. Thus there is more need for co-operative effort. They say also that with the growth of technology, the multiplication of means of communication and transportation, and the nationalization of economic affairs, problems that once were limited to the community and state become national. Size, they conclude, becomes the pattern of the times. For with businesses reaching a national market, labor spreading out to contend with management, and migrations of people from state to state and region to region, there must be a big government to serve and to regulate us. Thus their conclusion is that a Federal establishment must supplant the state and local units which sufficed in an earlier time. It can serve more efficiently, they believe, by centralization and size.

There are also the true humanitarians among the liberals. They, too, are perfectly sincere. They want people to live better in a nation whose resources are so opulent. The Federal government, they believe, can become the superministering angel.

The line between rational humanitarianism and sheer sentimentality is very thin indeed. The swelling heart overmasters the head. Love for the fellow man is expansive. But as Santayana once wrote in an essay on William James, the great pragmatist, "Love is very penetrating, but it penetrates to possibilities rather than to facts." The humanitarian urge gets out of hand. The pragmatic approach to public problems comes to be nothing more than an enlargement of the realm of unsettled questions.

It is a commendable practice to submit old traditions to periodic examination and challenge. But it does not free those who practice it from the need for logic and rational judgment. Some of the greatest of failures are those prompted by the best of intentions. Belief that we are on the verge of discovery is not discovery. Belief is important, but to cite Santayana again:

Believe rationally, holding what seems certain for certain, what seems probable for probable, what seems desirable for desirable, what seems false for false. . . . What is good is a clear head, aware of its resources, not a fuddled optimism, calling up spirits from the vasty deep.

Gentleness of soul is not always associated with keenness of mind. Charity, as Oscar Wilde remarked, "creates a multitude of sins." When applied by the clumsy and politically imbued hand of government it spawns a host of illusions.

Thus the sensitive liberal's antenna vibrates violently with every

demand from an ever-wanting public. He is not necessarily a
knave, he is naive. He is not delinquent, he is deluded. He is not
wayward, he is wayless.

There are also the liberal activists. What seems good to do
must be done at once. If there are mistakes, the sponsor can say
that his intentions were of the best. The reformer wants to "get
on with it," to "get moving." Those who counsel caution are dismissed with contemptuous references to "reaction." They are
"timid." They lack "imagination." They are sinners against the
gods of "progress."

Finally there are the rascally liberals in politics who neatly
tie together the humanitarians, the sentimentalists, and the activists and associate them with the selfish populace which seeks
something for nothing and uses this consolidated power for the
callous purpose of collecting votes and, with political success,
personal power.

This sort of liberal is quite willing to promote any scheme
which can create a mass appeal. Some of these are said to be
able to create more solutions than problems. There is really no
love for the needy in this ruthless type. But they become the
beneficiaries of their political capacity to weld together the good
intentions of some and the massive pretensions of others. In their
"dialogue" they boldly claim a monopoly of humanitarianism.

Those who oppose them are called the cold-hearted, the pur-
blind, the selfish, and the benighted of the past. In the firing lines
of politics these resourceful fellows are the ones with whom
the conservative must contend. For they are the binding elements
in political liberalism. They are the more wilful, practical people
who attain positions of greatest power.

I am not aware of the specific time at which those who now
claim the name "liberal" began to use the word in its current
context. It was not used in American politics in the days of
T. R. and Wilson. The word "progressive" served then. But its
early origins in British politics certainly show what a distortion

is represented in its application in American politics today. For early in the nineteenth century it meant an attachment to personal liberty. It was so understood in the days of John Stuart Mill. Gladstone used it as the name of the party he inherited from the old Whigs. But as time went on, British Liberals turned to broader measures of social reform and welfare. That is what Liberalism meant to Lloyd George.

The strains from which the ideology of the present version of American liberalism came are not difficult to trace. There were some importations from the British. Social security came from the British system inaugurated by Lloyd George. A few American individuals were interested in British Fabian socialism. And so far as American liberalism's economic theories are concerned, they are mostly a distortion of the philosophy of John Maynard Keynes.

But mostly our limitless liberal aspirations are the outgrowth of native beginnings in our states and local communities. These have been elevated to the status of Federal policies.

The economic interpretation of history which revolutionized American history-writing in the early years of the twentieth century has been taken over wholesale by liberal politicians to a degree that campaign appeals have come down to naked incitements of a material nature.

In the early years of the century business abused its power and facilitated a revolt which was one of the components of the Progressive political movement.

The influx of a new immigration had its impact. Unlike peoples of the original colonies who were dissenters imbued with Anglo-Saxon concepts of individual liberty, the more recent immigrants from continental Europe were habituated to authoritarian governmental and religious controls. Some carried the seeds of socialism. Immigrants in the Northwest and Midwest have influenced our life more than British Fabian importations. These settlers came before Fabianism was born and before Marx became an important influence in history. They held ideas of another sort of authoritarianism, shored up with well-established concepts of co-operative marketing and public ownership of utilities and a profound distrust of capitalism as it appeared in banking, railroads, and public utilities. The immense influence of Thorstein Veblen in American economic thought came from an embittered son of impoverished Scandinavian parents in Wisconsin.

Political trends follow patterns. The sins of business created a call for more government regulation. Leaders in "progressivism" looked for action at the state and then the Federal level. Theodore Roosevelt, ever the political opportunist, was quick to encompass this concept of enlarged Federal power in what he called his New Nationalism. While Woodrow Wilson adhered to his earlier constitutionalism in what he called his New Freedom, in his first term as President he achieved many of the objectives earlier promoted by the Progressives.

Then in 1917 came the tidal impact of war. Its paramount urgency required massive efforts which always enlarge centralized national authority and impose severe restrictions on individual liberty. Precedents established in emergencies became the goals of many in less troubled times.

Paralleling these influences was a trend toward more and more emphasis upon what is called social rather than individual responsibility. Ajustment or, as the word implies, conformity is the be-all and the end-all. In education a revision of earlier concepts was most prominent, and its product often was the hothouse bloom of "progressive education."

Tremendous mass influences exerted themselves. New means of communications and transportation drew the elements of the nation closer together. Physical uniformity replaced diversity as the geographical frontier receded.

Thus, most of the elements which found an ideological habitation and a name in liberalism were there well before the word itself came into use in the past thirty years.

The word "liberal" in its ideological sense has been seized by those who feel that everything is worth a trial. And what better instrument with which to experiment than the Federal government? Services should be standardized on a national scale. Also it is easier to get funds, with fewer questions, from the Federal establishment. Citizens fail to realize fully that the bureaucrat's wallet bulges with their cash, that Congressmen appropriate not remote figures but their hard-earned dollars.

A very prominent characteristic of the liberal's method is his appropriation of the word "science" to justify the application of his nostrums. "Statistics" and "facts" derived from government bureaus swarm through his "dialogue." This applies in the preparation of many, many bills and appropriation measures.

Much of the legislation which initiates various liberal programs is merely the expression of plausible, albeit noble, intentions. A real or fancied problem is spotted on the political horizon. A group or interest wants something which it says is a need. The liberal legislator, without conscious reflex, conceives that Federal money will meet the alleged need. He and his colleagues frame a statute. It is usually prefaced by an egregiously high-flown preamble, a legally meaningless statement of intent, before getting down to specifications. Votes are often lined up with the harshness of a drill sergeant. "Pressure," a nice word for threats, is applied. The bill is passed. A bureau or agency is created or a new duty placed upon an old one. An appropriation is given. And the job of applying the remedy to the alleged need is dumped upon the bureaucracy. And the liberals go on to other problems. They reason, if they reason at all, that they have solved the problem.

Thus programs are piled upon programs. The legislative sponsors have no idea of how their programs are going to operate. The bureaucrats must find a way—any way—or another bureaucracy may be piled upon them. Not all individual bureaucrats can be held responsible for the expensive contraption in which they are cogs. Many are no more to be censured than the children who infest a kitchen kept by an overgenerous cook.

These excesses become apparent when we consider the many items of legislation which have been proposed or enacted by successive Congresses and extensions of these measures through the operations of the massive Federal bureaucracy. They are based upon the concept of greater Federal power. Call it what you will—the New Deal, the Fair Deal, or the New Frontier—it is still a miscellany.

However we may argue about the repercussions of world-wide forces from which we have suffered, for years there prevailed a wave of opinion that the economy could not safely be entrusted to traditional economic laws and that more and more government action at the Federal level was essential. In the measures of relief and recovery which followed Roosevelt's inauguration in 1933 this prevailing political opinion was consummated in new forms of government intervention. Trends and forces, originated before 1920, were consolidated in an identifiable ideological concept which after 1935 became the controlling policies of the Democratic Party.

The programs of the Kennedy Administration represent a finalized form of liberalism. Perhaps the best concrete embodiment of liberalism is contained in the massive budget message of January, 1962, covering proposed expenditures for the fiscal year of 1963. As we contemplate this aggregation of government purposes and programs at an expenditure of more than $92 billion we may well ask how it should be described.

Is it socialism? No, although it contains traces of socialism. Current liberalism is not intent upon government ownership of industry, with the exception of the business of producing and distributing electric power. Liberalism is content with loading enterprise with repressive regulations and with taking away much of its income through taxation.

Is it the draft for the welfare state? No, although there is a lot of welfare in it. The danger to the individual's liberty is much more complex than either socialism or welfarism.

Is it a return to the planned economy which so many were hopeful of establishing in the 1930's? No, for to call this indiscriminate mass of benefits and projects a plan is to desecrate a good old word. If this aggregation of policies and programs springing from so many impulses, interests, and pressures gives the observer a sense of rugged grandeur, it arises from the wonder that so many liberals can believe so many things at the same time. To look upon these programs as the result of a unified plan is to believe that the accumulation of phonograph records, sweaters, soiled sneakers, tennis rackets, biology notebooks, petticoats, pennants, photographs, letters from home, hockey sticks, books, cigarettes, ash trays, toilet articles, stuffed dogs, athletic programs, and signs pilfered from restaurants which are scattered over the floor, chairs, bureau, phonograph, and bed in a college girl's room were placed there by an interior decorator.

Nobody planned all this. It was not created; it simply accumulated. There is nothing homogeneous about such a collection, no interrelationship among such items as subsidized transportation for city and suburban dwellers, the preservation of life among ducks and bears, school lunches, a National Board for the Promotion of Rifle Practice, rural telephones, subsidies, retraining workers displaced by automation, and aid to speculators in land through urban renewal. There is money not only for stopping juvenile delinquency but for the enlargement of prisons, for buying tombstones, and for studying the Greek Orthodox Church in Alaska. If we study this budget, the enactments of the liberal Congresses over the past two decades, and the utterances of Democratic Party leaders and their platforms, we find no consistent pattern except one—to enlarge Federal power.

While it is proper and inevitable that the Federal government assume a considerable responsibility for services formerly within the province of private organizations, the states, and local governments, the multiplication of these creations on the Federal level beyond a point at which they can be controlled by the Chief Executive and Congress not only narrows the liberty of the individual but ushers in a wide expropriation of the national income. It creates a vast bureaucracy which ultimately becomes a self-contained interest in itself—expensive, repressive, planless, and headless.

The creators of the superstate operate on two preposterous assumptions. One is that the citizenry is an obedient lot; the other, that bureaucrats are omniscient. Neither has ever appeared on this earth. Under the liberal's superstate there will always be an endless war of wits between the served and the servers, the regulated and the regulators. This is the natural condition under bureaucracy. It has been so in every large nation from China and ancient Egypt to modern France, where government ultimately came to be exercised by a bumbling bureaucracy pitted against the collective wits of the citizenry.

Our leviathan can hardly escape that tradition. It is good and bad intentions at work creating ill-considered and impossible tasks for government. The superstate is the tangible, amorphous product of our liberalism. The liberal supports and constantly adds to this vast accumulation of government powers, benefits, taxes, and regulations. And it is with this that free men must contend.

CHAPTER 7

Liberalism Captures a Party

A POLITICAL party is rarely created or completely altered by the relatively single-handed efforts and ingenuity of a leader. Instead, a party usually creates its leaders. A most remarkable exception to this rule was the transformation of the Democratic Party by Franklin D. Roosevelt in the middle and later 1930's.

A man born and nurtured in the atmosphere suitable to a conservative country gentleman, Roosevelt was by inheritance a Democrat of the old school of Tilden, Cleveland, and Wilson. He turned by nature to rural scenes. On the sidewalks of rowdy cities he harbored the outdoorsman's discomfort in alien surroundings and unfamiliar crowds. When he entered public life, it was as the choice of a rural county. As a state senator he fought against Tammany and the New York State city machines. Later, as governor, his majority was made secure by Republican votes, for many of New York's upstate Republicans were taken by the man's concern with rural problems and his proven opposition to city machines.

When he was nominated for President, Roosevelt's strength came from agricultural states. Delegations dominated by city bosses bitterly opposed him. And so it followed, in the campaign, that the nagging problem of agriculture came first. The Topeka speech forecast the New Deal farm policy and was instrumental in capturing the Middle Western states. Conservation was included in this category. Tariffs were treated in an oblique manner that satisfied neither high- nor low-tariff groups. Other lines of experimentation and reform were drawn in other speeches. Finally, Roosevelt pledged thoroughgoing conservatism on fiscal policy, relief from the national government only where states could not carry the burden, Federal provision of "temporary" work which foreshadowed the WPA and the CCC, co-operation within industry for "regularization and planning" which foreshadowed the NRA, and provision of "unemployment reserves."

Hence, in moving into the White House, Roosevelt believed firmly that if agriculture could be made prosperous, the industrial areas could revive as a consequence. There were, from the nature of the emergency, measures that had to be taken to save the economy. The banks had to be made secure. For the protection of investors, the issuance and sale of securities had to be regulated at the Federal level. And there had to be priority in relief to individuals in genuine need.

In 1935 Roosevelt with his lieutenant, Edward J. Flynn, took stock of their party. Flynn spoke as unchallenged leader of the powerful Democratic machine in the Bronx and, as such, was a great power in the City of New York. His problems and functions among his constituents were common enough—to be found with many leaders in other American cities of the time. Flynn, however, was unique. He presided over his area with astonishing efficiency and tolerated no dishonesty among his ward leaders and precinct captains. He allowed no personal familiarity on the part of his subordinates. The Bronx Democratic organization functioned with the precision of a well-generaled corps. In the first eight Roosevelt years Flynn was the strategist, Farley the technician.

Flynn and Roosevelt noted that, except for cities controlled by Democratic organizations and the traditional Democratic political system of the South, their party was nationally a rather ineffective force. They noted, too, that the Democratic Party had won the Presidency only because the great depression had temporarily upset the dominant Republican Party. They recognized that Wilson's two victories in a period of triumphant Republicanism, extending from 1896 to 1932, had hinged on Republican factionalism. In 1935 Flynn spoke to me of their decision:

"There are two or three million more dedicated Republicans in the United States than there are Democrats. The population, however, is drifting into the urban areas. The election of 1932 was not normal. To remain in power we must attract some millions, perhaps seven million, who are hostile or indifferent to both parties. They believe the Republican Party to be controlled by big business and the Democratic Party by the conservative South. These millions are mostly in the cities. They include racial and religious minorities and labor people. We must attract them by radical programs of social and economic reform."

Hence, the programs most powerfully urged by Roosevelt in the 1935 session of Congress incorporated Social Security, aimed essentially at urban wage-earners; the Holding Company Act, which undermined the strength of the big power companies; and the Wagner Act, which put government squarely behind the labor movement. Roosevelt's major messages and speeches took on a flavor of strong opposition to big business and business interests. Even Rexford Tugwell suggested that they were reminiscent of the utterances of William Jennings Bryan.

Welfare measures distributed government aid without much discrimination. The Far West and Northwest were wooed by Roosevelt's public power and reclamation projects. And the South, a prisoner of its one-party system, was taken for granted by a party majority which exalted Federal power. However, the South received its share of Roosevelt's attention by liberal policies. Negroes, first in the Northern cities and later in the South itself, were won over, almost to a man, not only by generous welfare measures but by the adoption of gestures against discrimination. The newly created C.I.O. plunged deeply into politics.

Thus, the man who was born to the heritage of a country

gentleman and who had dedicated nearly a quarter of a century to the cause of agriculture became within the space of a few years a leader and idol of the urban masses. A plentiful supply of patronage and Federal grants for housing, relief, and benefits to labor made secure control of great and growing urban centers. Intellectuals were won by Roosevelt's habit of "bold experimentation" and by his conversion to internationalism after 1937. The capacity he showed to adopt the ideas of a new and radical science of economics for the purpose of rationalizing his political policies won him great support in academic circles. And his amazing capacity to dramatize his policies and himself excited a public unable to discriminate among his projects and blinded by the excitement of a masterful show.

Roosevelt's war policies won him the support of national, racial, and religious groups who hated Hitler's Nazism. Gradually, organized labor became a telling force in many congressional districts and various states. While most of the great cities of the country had traditionally been dominated by Democratic machines, two of the great bastions of Republicanism, Chicago and Philadelphia, were ultimately to fall to the Democrats. In Presidential elections, state after state was won by Roosevelt and by Truman by piling up immense Democratic majorities in industrial centers while Republicans gained only in the suburbs and non-urban counties.

The transformation of the Democratic Party was established by the Roosevelt-Flynn strategy. The Democratic platform of 1960 was in every respect a manifesto of this reconstructed Democratic Party. In the election of that year John F. Kennedy emerged successfully as President and head of this neo-Rooseveltism.

For a time in the late 1930's Roosevelt toyed with the idea of boldly creating a new party dedicated to his policies. In this he hoped to bring Republicans who were also dedicated to the new Federal centralism into a common fold with liberal Democrats. But this idea was abandoned. The trade name "Democratic" was kept, but the substance of the party's heritage had undergone a metamorphosis. And with the change there came into use the word "liberal" to describe an ideology based upon the enlargement of the power of the Federal government and an abundance of welfare programs.

It was not difficult for many who had for years supported the Democratic Party to foresee that change and to deplore it. Some decided to remain in the party, hoping that through their influence the liberal trend might be halted. Others, like James A. Farley and John Nance Garner, found the old allegiance too hard to break.

My own decision was made in 1936. It was utter and irrevocable. I made it with the knowledge that the two-party system is the basic guarantee of individual liberty and constitutional government. The sudden shift in Roosevelt's policies and strategy in the 1935–1936 period meant to me the repudiation of Democratic Party principles of the past. Since I believed in supporting one of the two parties, I accepted the Republican Party as an alternative.

I cannot agree with those who cling loyally to the name "Democrat" when the substance has been dissipated.

CHAPTER 8

The Cult of Planning

ON the dedicatory page of Rexford G. Tugwell's book *The Industrial Discipline* [1] there appears this quotation from Francis Amasa Walker: ". . . the long debate of reason resulting in the glad consent of all."

This phrase embodies the hope of the sincere economic planner. It is based, just as socialism is based, upon the concept that under the aegis of government there could be an authority composed of an elite group which would assign to the producers of goods certain quotas, which by calculation would be approximately commensurate with the capacity and willingness of consumers to absorb such goods. To leave such calculations to private producers in a free market, the planner holds, inevitably results in dislocation and chaos. There will be overproduction and underconsumption and periodic depressions.

Three propositions are involved here. First, that the economy of a nation is so simple that the production and consumption of each of many types of products can be isolated one from the other and planned. This is based upon a misunderstanding of the inter-relations in an economic society. A man may need a new overcoat when the winter sets in. At home some repairs for the heating system may be necessary. A decision to satisfy these needs rests with him, with the members of his family, and with the

[1] New York: Columbia University Press, 1933.

47

condition of his finances. Such decisions, and hundreds of millions of them must be made every day, cannot be calculated because the conditions could not possibly be assessed by a government elite, however lavishly equipped with expensive computers.

The other two propositions are based upon preposterous assumptions which I noted earlier—that the planners are faultless and the citizens docile. To be without fault is not granted to any man, and even the commands of God have been subject to violations ever since Adam and Eve.

However, if, as is true in Soviet Russia and Communist China and as was true in Fascist Italy and Germany, a government appears which believes it can plan beyond a free market, obedience must be forced. Then there is planning, but at the cost of individual liberty.

The cult of planning has had an interesting history in this century. The form in which it was widely advocated in the 1930's originated long after Marx and at least two decades after the creation of the socialist Fabian Society in Britain.

In 1914, planning was adopted in Imperial Germany as a factor in waging total war. Its mastermind was Walter Rathenau, who in 1914 wrote a pamphlet, *Germany's Raw Materials Management*. It was published in many languages, and four hundred thousand copies reached the English-speaking world.

The United States introduced a measure of planning in the First World War through Bernard Baruch's War Industries Board. It adopted policies of priorities which caused some anguish in business circles and some fear in Congress. But it was liquidated after the Armistice.

In Russia, after finding his Bolsheviks fully in power, Lenin realized that the prophet Marx had provided plans only for revolution. Beyond revolution there were only useless generalities. Lenin said later, "I do not know of any socialist who has dealt with these problems. . . . We need a plan at once to give the masses a shining unimpeded example to work for."

Rathenau's plans supplied the immediate answer.

After the upset which put the British socialists in power in 1945, planning was found to be a useful tool. Prime Minister Attlee discovered his government to be overloaded with woolly-headed theorists. Schemes for nationalization faltered and elicited no enthusiasm from a war-wearied people.

When I visited Britain to observe the general election in 1950, I noted that there was much more talk of "planning" in the appeals of Labor than of orthodox socialism. Listening to Attlee in Edinburgh, I noted that he used the word at least a score of times. The restoration of the Conservatives came in 1951. But when I was over there again in 1955, the refrain was the major Labor issue again.

On the occasion of my next visit in 1959, the new leader of the Labor Party, Hugh Gaitskell, had shifted the refrain. His appeal was for more spending to increase the gross national product and thus fully to engage the labor force and provide more income to be taxed. This version of planning appeared in the liberal Democratic appeal in the United States in 1960.

In 1949, while the Labor Party was still in power, Professor John Jewkes, then of the University of Manchester, now of Oxford, brilliantly portrayed the shift from Marxism to planning in his book *Ordeal by Planning*.[2] He began by pointing out a number of commendable human aspirations embodied in the concept of central planning of the economy. These were: a desire to avoid the danger of mass unemployment which had followed wars in every nation which recognized free enterprise; a feeling, however naive, that men should be the masters of their economic affairs; and a belief that planning was a manifestation of the application to government policies of a scientific method, that if the government could plan economic affairs there could be greater increases in wealth, and that since great inequalities in wealth

[2] London: Macmillan and Co., 1949.

had always attended free enterprise a collective effort might avoid such unjust division of the fruits of industrial progress.

Summed up, these aspirations are born of a belief that it might be possible to harness technological and scientific improvements with the age-old human impulses such as humanitarianism, equality of opportunity, personal security, and economic stability.

But, as Jewkes shows in detail, these were completely and finally frustrated in the application of planning by the Labor government after 1945. The socialist dream of marrying socialism and liberty utterly failed. Step by step the Labor government moved toward coercion. Planning of the economy was ending in the planning of men's lives.

In the United States the cult of planning in the 1920's grew when many "intellectuals" found useful lessons in the experiments of the Soviet regime in Russia. According to the historical researches of Arthur Schlesinger, Jr.,[3] the cult of planning in the late 1920's drew a good deal of inspiration from the experiments of the Soviet regime in Russia:

In 1927 . . . a number of American liberals, among them John Dewey, Tugwell, Paul H. Douglas, and Stuart Chase, visited the Soviet Union. None was converted to the Communist theology or impressed by the exportability of the Communist solution. But several were struck by the demonstration in Russia of the power of the collective will. It was hard, Dewey wrote, "not to feel a certain envy for the intellectual and educational workers in Russia" because "a unified religious social faith brings with it such simplification and integration of life . . ." Tugwell, seeing Communism in Veblenian terms as "the experiment of running industry without the mechanism of business," felt himself inclining to the slightly sententious belief that "the humanly achieved industrial balance in Russia is more likely to attain the objective

[3] *The Crisis of the Old Order* (Boston: Houghton Mifflin Company, 1957). The three volumes of which this is the first are written from the standpoint of a dedicated planner. Collectively the history is called *The Age of Roosevelt*. In these books there is portrayed the growth of the cult, its early successes in the first Administration of Roosevelt, and its frustration after 1935.

of 'necessities for all before luxuries for any' than in our own competitive system."

Schlesinger goes on to describe at length the immense influence of the Soviet's experiments on many other American liberals.

The onset of the great depression fortified the doubts of such individuals about the capacity of the American economy under private ownership and management to maintain balance, even to survive. This lack of belief in the usefulness and permanence of an economic system operating under a free market is the most lasting impression I have of the thinking of the planners who gathered in such numbers in and around the Roosevelt Administration in its earlier years. While there, I had abundant opportunity to know them intimately and to hear them talk. The classical belief of the planners has been stated by Professor Joseph A. Schumpeter, at Harvard in those years, in his book, *Capitalism, Socialism and Democracy*. The businessman, he said, was on his way to extinction for these reasons:

Capitalism has once and for all performed a service which need not be repeated; the business man has failed to create defenses against political attack; his incentives are gone; capitalistic economy has created a hostility to its own social order.[4]

It was not unusual to find this sort of defeatism in an environment of a world-wide depression before which business leaders stood almost helpless. It is important to note, however, that the more socialistic European nations felt the impact of the depression along with the others.

Since Rexford G. Tugwell in those years attained the status of the foremost philosopher of economic planning and had considerable influence with the President, a statement of his position will be helpful in illustrating the aims of the case:

We possess every needful material for Utopia, and nearly everyone knows it: it is a quite simple conclusion in most minds

[4] Cited in Jewkes, *op. cit.,* pp. 18–19.

that control ought to be taken out of hands of people who cannot produce it from the excellent materials at their disposal.

It was my opinion then and it remains my opinion now that Tugwell was a dedicated and deadly serious man. I knew him well. He was my friend at Columbia University and I introduced him to Roosevelt. After his visit to Russia he was temporarily encouraged to believe that there was a solution to what he regarded as industrial chaos. He was profoundly depressed after the economic crash in 1929 but recovered hope after meeting Roosevelt. His hopes declined, however, as Roosevelt veered away from planning in 1936.

When, in 1933, the Agricultural Adjustment Administration, the National Recovery Administration, and the Tennessee Valley Authority were created, national economic planners joyously believed that they were witnessing the dawn of a planning era. But the Supreme Court made short shrift of the plans for agriculture and business. Roosevelt then shifted his attention to the reconstruction of the Democratic Party according to his shrewd concepts of political expediency. He lost interest in all economic planning except in the production of electric power and what was then regarded as a small Federal enterprise in rural electrification. His economic policies from 1936 to the outbreak of the war were capricious and often mutually contradictory.

The lamentations of the planners over this change are duly recorded in the historical writings of Rexford G. Tugwell and Arthur Schlesinger, Jr.

The onset of the war in 1939 placed a heavy responsibility on the once-styled "decadent" American industry, first in helping the nations opposed to Hitler and later in our own participation. The spectacular capacity of American free enterprise met that test. Even the development of the atomic bomb was carried out under contracts by various American industrial companies. The final victory, so largely due to the role of the United States as "the arsenal of democracy," should have silenced the planners.

But as the war approached its end in 1945, a bill was introduced in Congress which was clearly a revival of the concept of planning. It was called "The Full Employment Bill." The purpose of the bill as stated in the preamble was:

To the extent that continuing full employment cannot otherwise be achieved, it is the further responsibility of the Federal government to provide such volume of Federal investment and expenditure as may be needed to assure continuing full employment.

Under the terms of the bill the President, with the assistance of a Council of Economic Advisers, would state annually what the state of employment would be and what would be needed to assure jobs for all, with government help where needed. This, of course, assumed clairvoyant powers of prophecy in a government bureau. It also assumed that government spending could assure the stated number of jobs at once and wherever needed. These were fantastic assumptions, as should have been apparent from the experience of the 1930's when, despite increased government spending, unemployment increased from 1936 to 1939.

It should be noted that the very economic seers who had helped prepare this bill and who provided the arguments for it were at the same time predicting an enormous increase in unemployment immediately after the war. Never has a prediction projected by allegedly scientific economists been so egregiously wrong.

Fortunately, under the vigorous leadership of Senator Taft the bill was whittled down to a simple fact-gathering and opinion-uttering affair, with a Council of Economic Advisers under the President and a Joint Economic Committee in Congress. These two have periodically issued reports, usually under a Republican President and a Democratic Congress, the one sharply disagreeing with the other. About the only effect on employment these have had has been the hiring of a few economists with varying points of view.

Planning as it worked out in Britain under the Labor Party

from 1945 to 1951 revealed itself, as Jewkes so well shows, as a state of utter confusion among the planners. It was not scientific. It failed to produce prosperity or economic stability. It was the enemy of individual liberty. And it infected the nation with a moral sickness from which recovery has been difficult and protracted.

But planning has reappeared under the Kennedy Administration in a new dress, with new catchwords and with equally futile and pernicious threats to the economy.

CHAPTER 9

Neoplanning in the 1960's

THE superstate, as envisioned in the Democratic platform of 1960, in the speeches of Candidate Kennedy in that year,
and in the programs he has recommended as President, cannot
be characterized as a plan. But there are two characteristics of
planning which have reappeared in the New Frontier. One of
them is the concept of stimulating the rate of economic growth
through government spending, and the other is government activities designed to create a vast network of Federally owned and
operated electric power facilities. Neither is new. The first was
activated in Roosevelt's second term but brought out clearly in
the originally proposed Full Employment bill in 1945. The second
is merely a renewed effort to achieve plans vigorously promoted
before the Second World War by Roosevelt and Secretary of the
Interior Ickes. These rusty weapons of an old battlefield have
been recovered and by the magic chemistry of semantics made
to do for another battle.

Growthmanship

There was a period, just before the onset of World War II,
when we were told that the American economy was "mature."
There was, it was said, no further need for venture capital by the
big corporations in expanding their productive capacity. Private
savings were inert and stagnant and needed to be channeled off

by taxation. New industries must be helped by Federal grants from such revenues. These expressions of theory were fully exploited in the hearings of the Temporary National Economic Committee in 1939–1940.

Twenty years later liberals preferred a concept of the attainment and acceleration of growth based upon the power of government, planned by a central decision-making authority according to a percentage of increase.

Collateral to this thesis is a concept which gained wide acceptance in 1960 and which was persuasively presented in Professor John K. Galbraith's popular book, *The Affluent Society*. The country was flooded by pamphlets, speeches, and commentaries in that decisive year. The thesis held that the public was consuming too much of the "unessential," such as automobiles, television sets, gadgets, beauty preparations, and the like. That was called "affluence." By contrast, it was said, the public "sector"—i.e., government construction, welfare benefits, and educational facilities—was neglected. "Private affluence and public squalor," somebody said.

We could not expect that a generation of middle-aged politicians and academicians could look back to the thesis of the "mature" economy school of the TNEC days of 1939–1940 and realize how the "new" theory of growthmanship is based upon a completely different concept of individual behavior. At that time when these liberals were twenty years younger it was said that citizens were too thrifty with their "poisonous" savings. Now they are spendthrifts!

But whatever may be the crime—loose spending or tight saving—the punishment is the same. The criminal shall be mulcted of his money by taxation.

The government statistic, Gross National Product, is used as a measurement. But, as Dean W. Allen Wallis of the School of Business of the University of Chicago says, ". . . the basic figures of the G.N.P.—and ours are the best in the world—involve liberal use of estimation and guesstimation, of interpolation and extrapolation, of approximation and adjustment."

Wallis further points out that there are at least six ways of measuring economic growth. These are: percentage rates of increase in G.N.P. adjusted to price changes; real G.N.P. per capita; industrial production; output for unit of capital and labor combined; and real disposable income per capita.

In presenting the argument that natural and traditional processes of growth are inadequate to the "new" age, the zealots, even the 1960 Democratic candidate for President, use the patently unreliable method which has been called a "numbers game." What span of years are you going to use to determine a rate of growth? A favorite of the exponents of growthmanship is a comparison of figures between 1947 and 1953 with the figures from 1953 to 1959. This, Wallis says, is "unwise, unwary, or unscrupulous." I would add purely political, for its purpose is to contrast growth under Truman with growth under his successor. But 1947 was a year of war reconversion, and therefore growth was small; 1953 was the top of the Korean war boom, and therefore of large volume. However, starting with that high rate of G.N.P. in 1953 and ending in 1959, an average year, the rate of growth would be small. Thus, says Wallis, "you pick your party and then pick your years." But when those who advocate this attempt to compare the U. S. rate of growth during these spans of years with the rates in other countries, the nonsense becomes utterly compounded. For economic activity in one country never can be compared with those of other countries during the same years. Japan and Germany were starting from next to nothing. Russia went from the vast frustration of war to recovery in peace.

Another fallacy was added to the congeries of irresponsible delusions and tricks of the growth-by-government-spending thesis. The G.N.P., even if it were accurate, would be the wrong way to measure real growth. For it is a dollar measurement, a gross measurement even when it is adjusted to the changes in the dollar value. It does not account for growth in quality of product. Consider automobile tires as an example. They now cost only a little more than in 1930, but they give several times as many miles of use.

And so it is with every product which builds in the results of invention and refinement. A nation's economy could progress if its rate took account of only the increase in population, merely by adding quality and longer wear to what it consumes.

Another vital flaw in the argument for greater growth by large diversion from the "private" to the "public" sector by government spending is this: government spending primarily constitutes purchases. Such purchases are not production. The government merely takes over goods produced in the private economy. To create such goods there must be plants, equipment, raw materials, and personnel. And those requirements to meet government purchases must be taken from the savings of the people in the form of investment. The exactions made through taxation and, if there is a deficit, by inflation destroy those savings. So government spending must be at the cost of real economic growth.

The official line of the British Labor Party as stated in 1959 by Hugh Gaitskell was growthmanship. This he offered as a substitute for the socialism and central planning of the Attlee era. It would merely shift the emphasis from the ownership of the means of production to the confiscation of income and its diversion into the "public sector." That this would involve coercion is admitted by Galbraith. For his remedy for the inevitable inflation that ensues under prodigious government spending would be price and wage controls.

The growthmanship theory is a wholly unjustified extension of the theories of Keynes. Those who advocate spending in anticipation of growth are, as Colin Clark says, paying an exaggerated respect to Keynes's doctrines after they have ceased to be of primary importance. For Keynes over and over said that he was suggesting spending, even at the cost of inflation, to fit such conditions of depression as prevailed in the 1930's. The efforts of his disciples to continue such spending after the emergency passed were strongly opposed in the final years of his life. It is a case of the sorcerer's apprentices, who can turn on the flood of spending but lack the master's skill or resolution to turn it off after its purpose has been served.

Toward a Federal Monopoly of Electric Power

Before the 1920's, the Federal government produced only a slight amount of electric power in its reclamation projects. But even before that, it had been the dream of socialists here and in Europe that the nationalization of industry should begin with interconnecting government utilities such as railroads, telegraph and telephone lines, and power production and transmission. Therefore, it was not strange that Lenin, seeking to find practical means of implementing the Marxian dream, hit upon a monopoly of electric power as early as 1920. Acording to Sidney Webb, the new dictator wrote to Krzhizhanovsky in that year:

Couldn't you produce a plan (not a technical but a political scheme) which would be understood by the proletariat? For instance, in 10 years (or 5?) we shall build 20 (or 30 or 50?) power stations covering the country with a network of such stations, each with a radius of operation of say 400 versts (or 200 if we are unable to achieve more) . . . We need such a plan at once to give the masses a shining, unimpeded prospect to work for: and in 10 (or 20) years we shall electrify Russia, the whole of it, both industrial and agricultural. We shall work up to God knows how many kilowatts or units of horsepower.[1]

Despite the grand plans of the Soviet, this brainstorm of Lenin failed of accomplishment. By 1960 the Soviet had built only 62,000 miles of transmission lines. In the United States, private

[1] Jewkes, *op. cit.*, pp. 2, 3.

companies and government had built a total of 304,000 miles. The average annual use of electricity in the United States in 1960 was 3,927 kilowatt-hours per capita; in the Soviet, it was 300.

In the United States in the 1920's there was considerable controversy over who should complete and operate the Muscle Shoals Dam on the Tennessee River, a World War I installation. But this failed to be decided until, under Roosevelt, Muscle Shoals became the basis of the TVA. Some American socialists who called themselves gradualists decided that their ends could not be accomplished merely through support of the Socialist Party. In a socialist publication there appeared an article by H. Stephen Rauschenbush. Rauschenbush is the son of a noted German-born Christian Socialist professor of theology, Walter Rauschenbush. The younger Rauschenbush stated his view, that socialism would never accomplish its purpose of nationalizing all industry. But by infiltrating the government with individuals who would work toward a step-by-step process, much more could be done. And so he equipped himself as an expert in coal, oil, and electricity, which he regarded as prime factors in industrial life. He served in several official and unofficial bodies for some years. In the article to which I have referred, he said: "One good man with his eyes, ears, and wits about him, inside the department [of government] . . . can do more to perfect the technique of control over industry than a hundred men outside."

And so he entered government during the New Deal period, first in the State of Pennsylvania and then in the Department of the Interior under Secretary Ickes in 1939, where he remained until 1947.

Secretary Ickes himself was not a socialist. But his zeal for government ownership of electric power production was undeniable. When he was Secretary of the Interior several of the great Federal dams were built. In the laws authorizing these installations there always appeared what is known as the "preference clause." This provided that preference in the sale of power from such Federal installations should always be given to public power agencies and co-operatives. In other words, while a private company might make a contract to purchase a certain amount of Federal power from such installations, its supply could always be preempted at the termination of the contract by either a municipally owned system or by a co-operative. In one manifesto to his employees, Ickes told the Interior bureaucracy not only to favor government power but actively to go out and help form public power systems in the states, cities, and counties.

In 1936 the Rural Electrification Administration was created. This ostensibly was to provide Federal funds at a low interest rate to co-operatives who would then serve subsidized electric power to rural residents who could not be economically served by private companies. This has grown enormously in the years since.

It is not strange, then, that the bureaucracy of the Interior Department is still determined to enlarge the area of Federal power production and control. Indeed, it has come to be a sacred tradition.

However, during the Eisenhower Administration these bureaucrats were kept, however reluctantly, within a new policy of partnership, which favored co-operative activities in building new installations by the government public power agencies and investor-owned private companies. But the Ickes administration left behind several intraregional tieups or "grids," linking these installations one with the other. There was the TVA, the Bonneville Power Administration, and the Southwestern Power Administration. There were also plans for a Missouri Basin Administration and a Northeast Power Administration.

Under the Rural Electrification Administration the Federal government still lends money to rural electric co-operatives at a rate of 2 per cent. This money now costs the taxpayers of the nation nearly twice as much. This is a huge subsidy for supplying a need which no longer exists.

The coming of atomic power has become a glittering temptation for nationalized power. Several bills have been introduced in successive sessions of Congress to accomplish this end. In the early installations for war purposes the expense was so great that no single company could afford to build these plants. However, Congress has refused to approve of anything that suggests nationalized atomic power for the production of electricity.

The growth of government power production—Federal and municipal—is shown by its percentages of total production of kilowatt-hours generated. It was 4.9 billion in 1932. In 1959 it was 161.3 billion. Much of this is from steam plants.

The National Resources Advisory Committee, sponsored by Messrs. Kennedy and Johnson, called for "immediate attention to the economic necessity of national transmission lines." Stewart L. Udall, the Secretary of the Interior, had been one of the foremost members of Congress who consistently supported Federal power expansion. He immediately appointed a "task force" to study the question. But apparently little study was necessary, because the Interior bureaucracy had bided its time for an Administration favorable to its plans. This task force spoke of the "exciting promise" of long-distance power transmission. It would play a great role in stimulating industrial development in West Virginia, Pennsylvania, South Dakota, Montana, and Alaska. The inclusion of Alaska in this "gosplan" probably came from the hope that Congress might approve of a proposal to build a mammoth dam on the Yukon River designed to generate three times the power now produced at Grand Coulee.

The inter-tie of existing Federal operations would link many such units as the Bonneville Power Administration in the Northwest, the Upper Colorado project, the Federal installations in California, the Southwest Power Administration, the Missouri Valley, the TVA, the Northeast and St. Lawrence generating plants. This would create a nation-wide Federal system with great potential to control and redistribute much of American industrial life.

Altogether, the old dream of socialists and planners to nationalize the production and transmission of electric power as a major step to Federal control of all industry is clearly an objective of the Kennedy Administration.

CHAPTER 10

The Malign Growth of Bureaucracy

THIS sinister title should be clarified, for most members of the vast army of our government servants are worthy individuals. The source of danger is not the character of these persons but the system in which they serve. That system arises inevitably from the superstate which is shapeless, planless, unreformed, uninformed, internally inconsistent, heterogeneous, and sprawling.

To trace the rise of bureaucracies from ancient China and Imperial Rome to the Bourbon kings and Prussia under Frederick the Great would serve little purpose other than to underline the dismal experience men have always had with this monstrous child of excessive government.

Our own times offer modern examples. In Russia the Bolsheviks inherited an immense and tyrannical bureaucratic framework from the Czars and fleshed it with Soviet administration. The shortcomings of this ponderous, oppressive system have been the targets of all manner of criticism from the Central Committee and Party Congresses.

The multitudinous activities of continental European nations have long been operated by bureaucrats, "functioning by the book," under central ministry directives with occasional deviations induced by bribes. Individual judgments on everything from education to customs become unnecessary. Routine sets in and becomes the sole guide to decisions. Addiction to government by ukase dulls intelligence, deadens imagination, and freezes initiative.

The British permanent civil service is quite properly admired by those Americans concerned with the study and training of administrators. But its fine quality would be impossible to realize in the immense operations of government in the United States. The highly trained, carefully selected British civil servant is utterly without political concerns. He serves with equal devotion a Conservative or a Labor minister. In Britain the problems created by numbers are fewer than here, and the patterns of activity have been developed over a long period. Moreover, the civil servant is closer to the minister of his department who is a member of Parliament and is closer to the source of ultimate authority than our civil service personnel, bureau chiefs, and Cabinet officers. Currents of public opinion reach him and inform him.

However, inefficiency and bungling have crept into even this tested system with venerable arrangements. Crabgrass and stubborn weeds take root even in English lawns.

Only in the past two or three decades have Americans given much thought to the dangers presented by a huge Federal bureaucracy. Before, concern with and agitation against the "spoils system" occupied our attention.

After the Civil War, reformers most actively opposed the practice of giving jobs for party service. This created a deep fissure in the dominant Republican Party. Then, in the wake of a wide emotional reaction after the assassination of President Garfield in 1881 at the hand of a disappointed office-seeker, the reformers seized their opportunity and pressed Congress to enact legislation providing for Federal civil service reform. This "merit system" provided for examination for Federal positions, with tenure dependent, so it was believed, upon proficiency rather than political favor. Succeeding Presidents by executive order swept more and more Federal employees into the civil service categories, in most cases filling new agencies with political appointees before gathering them into the security of tenure. Under the administrations of Franklin D. Roosevelt, the many new agencies which were created added large numbers to the Federal payroll, and in nearly all cases Congress provided that they should be covered by civil service. Over the years tens of thousands whose ideology, politics, and sympathies were in line with those of the Roosevelt Administration found this shelter in the bureaucracy.

The push of Chief Executives, the promises of political platforms, and the reckless manner in which Congress has passed new functions to government are responsible for the growth of the monstrous body of office-holders which wields so much power over all of us.

In the first eight years of the Roosevelt regime, the nonmilitary civilian employees of the Federal government increased from 502,000 to 786,000. By 1952, the final full year of the Truman Administration, the number had hit 1,226,000. During the war and seven postwar years civilian employment in military establishments rose from 256,000 to 1,332,000. This figure has remained well over a million during the years of the Cold War.[1]

When President Eisenhower took office, one of his basic promises was to cut back the bureaucracy. His efforts yielded no reduction but, as compared with the years preceding under Roosevelt and Truman, he held the line rather well. In 1953 civilian, nonmilitary employment was 1,226,000. In 1960 it was 1,351,000.

The data are not complete for 1961, but the rise has noticeably been resumed under the liberal policies of President Kennedy. From 1960 figures to the latest figures for 1961 the rise in civilian, nonmilitary employment was 42,000. With new agencies and services enacted by Congress, the rise is certain to continue at a steep rate.

The growth of bureaucracy in the United States comes into

[1] These figures, as well as those immediately following, are official compilations by the U.S. Civil Service Commission, which carry back to 1816.

clearer focus when we consider certain specific departments. In 1932 there were 4,836 employees in the Department of State. In 1940 there were 6,302. But by dumping into the State Department many war-created agencies, originally designed to be temporary, there were 24,628 by 1950. And in 1961 there were 38,792.

The Department of Agriculture has grown prodigiously under liberal policies since 1933. In 1961 its employees numbered 102,557, more than triple the 1932 figure. The Department of the Interior numbered 20,486 in 1932; 59,369 in 1953. Although it was cut back under Eisenhower it is swiftly regaining its former bulk.

The Department of Health, Education and Welfare went into business in 1953, gathering within it several formerly independent agencies. It started with 35,408 employees. Its personnel has since doubled.

Another manifestation of the bureaucracy has been its penetration into the states and communities across the nation and into many, many nations around the world. Those who have seen the city of Washington grow with the bureaucracy since the days of Hoover know only a part of its spread. Only 15 per cent of the employees of five departments—Agriculture, Commerce, Interior, Health, Education and Welfare, and Treasury—work in the District of Columbia. Eighty-five per cent of their ranks are scattered through the states and in foreign lands. Vast and often palatial new buildings constructed during the past twenty-five years house the proliferation. And employees are given mobility everywhere through great pools of automobiles and buses. Traveling costs alone have reached figures in the tens of millions of dollars. In some states the number of Federal employees exceeds that of state and local agencies.

A number of circumstances have transformed a group of generally worthy individuals into a mass power which threatens the integrity and permanence of free institutions. One is the tendency of bureaucracy to survive and to grow. The way to promotion of supervisory or executive bureaucrats is to acquire more subordinates. Thus, more money and more personnel are always requested than the work-load justifies. By its very nature and widespread structure, bureaucracy assures its survival and its growth.

Bureaucrats, with adequate time and a host of assistants, exercise great political power through lobbying among members of Congress. Congressmen and Senators can gain much for their states or districts by currying favors from a bureau or department. The bureaucrat can line up votes for more appropriations in return for such favors. And, since the bureaucracy sprawls over the nation, its members can whip up demands in local communities which create pressures on Senators and Congressmen. The Army Corps of Engineers is a master of such activity.

When the people exercise their now semisovereign power to employ a President they place him in more or less of a prison, for the President cannot effectively control such an immense establishment as the Federal bureaucracy. His Cabinet members and bureau chiefs, too, share his captivity.

As an example, observe the President's limitations in effectuating military policies. There has grown up between the President and his professional military leaders a civilian blanket consisting of the office of the Secretary of Defense. There is the Secretary himself. Under his immediate charge is a thick civilian layer of functionaries—about three thousand people responsible to the Deputy Secretary, seven Assistant Secretaries, and the Director of Research and Engineering. President Kennedy before the Cuban Affair made this bureaucratic insulation more impervious by another civilian blanket of various and sundry assistants and advisors, drawn from the Harvard Yard and M.I.T., self-styled experts in military and global matters. At that time the military commanders of the services simply could not effectively penetrate to their Commander in Chief.

Finally, the bureaucrat, however well-intentioned he may be at the outset of his career, later falls into an impersonal, machine-like routine. He is not directly responsible to the people with whom he is in contact and whom he is designed to serve. There is little chance of appeal from a citizen to the superiors of a bureaucrat who has been unfair and arbitrary. Try sometime to appeal by letter to such a superior. Perhaps after weeks or months a routine letter will come back written by an associate of the offending bureaucrat.

The less his intelligence and human understanding, the more arbitrary the bureaucrat's decisions. For he is operating with the shield of law and innumerable directives of higher bureaucrats. His life may become a perpetual contest with the public, but he "has his orders."

CHAPTER 11

The Narcotic of Authority

IT IS logical to assume that a superstate demands at its head a superstatesman. But even if there were individuals supreme in knowledge, in foresight, and in judgment, none of the methods yet devised assures selection of such men as heads of the state. The accident of inheritance cannot guarantee this leadership. Nor can a council of elders. Nor a democracy or republic in which the caprice of politics tosses leaders to the top.

These people are subject to an inherent weakness in men: they are allergic to the narcotic of power. We see this in parents, those possessed of great fortunes, corporation executives, military commanders, union leaders, and those entrenched in politics. Ralph Roeder accounts for some of the excesses committed by the Duc de Guise when he attained supreme power in France under Francis II: "Time had told, time and the uses of power which, like a mould, takes in all temperaments and turns out the same prototypes." [1]

What are the symptoms of this transformation? The leader is under a compulsion to believe utterly in the wisdom of his decisions. He rebuffs advice. He develops a suspicion of the motives of those who disagree with him. Gradually he drives away all except compliant associates. He becomes a receptacle for flattery.

[1] *Catherine de' Medici and the Lost Revolution* (New York: Viking Press, 1937), p. 196.

He resorts to threats and force to sustain his directives. He is subject to trivial caprice. Finally his faculties are corroded and reasonable judgment is lost.

The memoirs of Caulaincourt, faithful Master of Horse under Napoleon, reveal the effect of power upon the Emperor. When Napoleon decided to move into Russia Caulaincourt attempted to dissuade him. From two years' experience in Russia Caulaincourt warned that in Moscow the autumn winter "explodes like a bombshell." Napoleon's amazing reply was that he knew better. Moscow's weather was no worse than Fontainebleau. This blunder cost an army of six hundred thousand men.

Hitler, too, suffered from this fatal certitude. The marrow of his power was derived from his native genius as an orator. The first groups he addressed were an assortment of sordid, psychotic, perverted, and villainous people who became the nucleus of his party. Later vast throngs gathered to hear him. He dwelt upon the real or imagined sufferings of his listeners, their bitterness, their racial and religious prejudices. He elevated their emotions by panegyrics on the puissance of the German race and its potential supremacy in the world. Ultimately the man was the captive of his message and his excited audience. Supreme political power induced him to believe that he was an omniscient military strategist. Generals, admirals, and statesmen were overruled, brushed aside, and often summarily dismissed or assassinated. A superb military machine, brilliantly trained in its art, was burned out on the big maps in the war rooms in Berlin. Ultimately no one remained at his side but Goebbels, his mistress, and a few who had lived his wild dream with him.

Ralph Roeder's account of the rise and fall of Savonarola in *The Man of the Renaissance* reveals the friar's bizarre ascendancy:

When he treated the sermon as a logical exercise the crowd cooled, and with the quick instinct of the orator he reverted to the rhapsodies which fired it. . . . A contagious anxiety passed from the preacher to the crowd and from the crowd to the preacher, and the flock, stirring uneasily . . . undulated to his prompting and multiplied his marshalling will. . . . He knew the solace of a vast fellow-feeling and an intoxicating illusion of personal power that touched the very quick of life; and that sensation, once known, he could never forego . . . it became a question whether his eloquence was the result of his convictions or his convictions of his eloquence.[2]

Ultimately prophecy followed prophecy. Denunciation became the voice of divine vengeance. Then Savonarola ventured too far. He promised a miracle, and it did not materialize. That broke the spell. Laughing, the crowd turned against him. His political control of Florence collapsed, and his enemies closed about him and carried him to the stake.

In a modified degree, and despite the care with which our constitutional system hedges our chief executives, the narcotic of power has gained a hold on some of our Presidents. Woodrow Wilson is a striking example. Authority was not strange to him, for he had presided over Princeton and occupied the governorship in New Jersey before gaining the White House. When he reached the White House, as he said in a lecture on the Presidency in 1908, he was able to make of the office whatever his personal capacity might create. The excessive effect of authority became apparent just before the elections in 1918, when by identifying a victory for his party with a mandate for himself he demanded the election of a Democratic Congress. Wilson's intimates say they questioned his decision. But he persisted and failed.

The war ended, and Wilson sailed to Europe to shape the terms of peace. The vast emotional reception accorded him in the capitals of Europe stimulated his determination to go it alone. Already he had rejected co-operation with experienced leaders of the opposition party and had taken with him only a delegation of intimates and subordinates. One by one even these were cast aside, including Lansing, House, and Hoover. Back in the United States

[2] (New York: The Viking Press, 1935), p. 24.

he rejected all compromise in the Senate against the urgings of Democratic leaders. He took the case to the country armed only with his eloquence. His physical faculties failed him and his great crusade came to an end.

I have already noted the transformation of the measurably modest and reasonable Franklin D. Roosevelt after the great successes with his program in 1933, in the Congressional elections of 1934, and his re-election in 1936. Certain details are essential to explain this change of character.

As time passed there appeared symptoms that the narcotic of power was working within Roosevelt. In 1932 he listened to advice. I wrote in 1939:

No one respected more than he the right of others to their own opinions. No one seemed less likely to be overwhelmed by the illusion of his own rectitude. . . . Nor did I foresee the growth of that irritable certitude that led Roosevelt to ascribe self-interest or cowardice or subtle corruption or stupidity to people who questioned the rightness of his impulses to action. . . . I could not imagine that a growing identification of self with the will of the people would lead him on to an attempted impairment of those very institutions and methods which have made progressive evolution possible in this country.

But then, I did not reckon with what seemed, in a United States which cried out for action and assertion, perhaps the most irrelevant political axiom wise men through the ages had ever devised. I had not yet learned that no temperament, however fluid, is immune to the vitrifying effect of power. . . . The failing is that of all men, not of one man.[3]

As the early months in his exalted office stretched into years Roosevelt became more and more insulated from those who would question his courses of action, offer blunt advice, or differ with him. Most of his visitors, seeking something from him, were ready with studied compliments. He developed methods of reassuring himself of his own preconceptions. Those around him

3 *After Seven Years* (New York: Harper and Brothers, 1939), pp. 396–97.

helped to close windows of his mind. Eventually he himself was slamming them shut. Sincere men with strong principles could not go along with Roosevelt's changed temperament and departed. The sycophants tarried. Then a difference of opinion became the mark of an enemy.

Roosevelt concluded his campaign for re-election in 1936 with words which shocked a great many thoughtful people:

Never before in all our history have these forces been so united against one candidate as they stand today. They are unanimous in their hate for me—and I welcome their hatred.

I should like to have it said of my first Administration that in it the forces of selfishness and of lust for power met their match. I should like to have it said of my second Administration that in it these forces met their master.

Two bitter defeats came to Roosevelt soon after. His attempt to reorganize the Supreme Court was beaten in Congress. And a year later his move to "purge" the United States Senate of dissenters in his own party was totally frustrated.

The coming of World War II gave him an opportunity to exercise unusual "emergency" powers. International agreements became a special province. The disastrous agreements which Roosevelt made on his own responsibility at Casablanca, Cairo, Teheran, and Yalta are too well known in their nature and consequences to be detailed here. They were demonstrations of judgment and moral rectitude frayed and worn by long exercise of power.

I cannot conclude this account of the narcotic of power upon those who exercise it without telling of a comment made to me by the famous historian Charles A. Beard. He made it in 1948 in his home in the Connecticut hills, surrounded by books which chronicled the behavior of men throughout history. As a student I had been powerfully influenced by his exposition of the virtues of nationalism. Later he had followed the development of Roosevelt's policies with such enthusiasm that he collaborated on a book entitled *The Future Comes*. He had ardently supported the efforts of Roosevelt to reorganize the Supreme Court. But the coming of the war with its aftermath had not only disillusioned Beard with Roosevelt but had revised many of his earlier views on centralized personal and governmental power. Speaking of the fight over the Court reorganization in 1937 and the people who had opposed it, he said, "They were right and I was wrong. They knew their man."

Those who, under the name of liberalism, humanitarianism, and other alluring terms, strive to create a Federal leviathan either do not appreciate perils attendant upon vesting such power in a man at the top and in the bureaucracy under him, or they think they see in this the wave of the future. In any case they would build a superstate in which there can never be supermen to direct it.

CHAPTER 12

The Tyranny of Minorities

ONE of the most treasured American ideals is our belief in a classless society. For that reason many of us view with profound regret and apprehension the transformation of our electorate into a congeries of groups, each intent upon exacting from the aggregate of the nation its own special privileges, immunities, and benefits. In the face of this disquieting fact, many of the expressions so firmly embedded in the dialect of our past linger on in our language without meaning or substance—such expressions as "democracy," "equality," and "government of the people, for the people, and by the people."

There are minorities which originate in race and religion. There are also sectional minorities. And there are minorities created by occupational interests. These, however, have always existed and, so long as the overriding priority of the public interest is strictly observed, are not inimical to our national unity and purpose.

The superstate, however, creates many new minorities. Special privileges, immunities, and benefits of various kinds create such groups and cement their members into great sources of political power. As they grow, their demands increase with their capacity to make exactions for more and more privileges, immunities, and benefits.

The liberalism of this generation has strengthened such groups and has yielded more and more to them. However, this process is not new. Special treatment for business interests, which extends as far back as Alexander Hamilton's plea for aid to the manufacturers and the first tariff measures, proliferated to the point at which the Republican Party became their servant. Following the Civil War the power of the veterans was strong enough to sway at least one Presidential election. The opposition to business at the turn of the century gave rise to the use of the derogatory term "special interests." This term of reproach lingered in political debate long after its origins had been forgotten. Presidents Roosevelt and Truman were most adept at using such contemptuous terms in their oratory even while they were busy creating a flock of new special interests.

Consider a few examples of these privileged groups which have grown into pressure organizations of great importance. The labor unions were a relatively minor factor in national politics until the Wagner Act of 1935 gave them a very advantageous position. For a considerable period the "farm bloc" in Congress and the pressure of farm organizations in the states wielded great influence on national policies. Wars create veterans and Congress provides pensions and other benefits. Thereafter the organized efforts of veterans intensify their pressure for more. Tax exemptions and advantages create organizations of the groups thus benefited. From a small beginning in the 1930's government aid to provide electricity to remote farms has grown into one of the most powerful pressure organizations in the nation, the National Rural Electric Cooperatives Association. The National Education Association, created as a means of improving education through better teachers, has become a potent lobby which presses Congress for Federal aid to schools and teachers.

One of the most recent manifestations of the efforts of political leaders to create a vast agency of power has been the drive to provide medical aid to the elderly. The potential of this group increases as improvements in medical care and the practice of earlier retirement create a senior and mostly retired population of approximately seventeen million. These senior citizens, so many of them with time on their hands, have been most important factors in the politics of many states. Now, however, we are witnessing a concerted effort by the liberals to weld this immense voting power into a tremendous special interest.

These groups, once created, have been eagerly exploited by politicians, for they offer to candidates the vast advantage of getting votes in great packages.

The most powerful auxiliary of the liberal Democrats is in organized labor. For more than a generation the unions followed a policy proclaimed by Samuel Gompers: that the best interests of labor required that the unions remain aloof from actual alignment with either party. He urged wage earners to vote for candidates who would promise to respond to the interests of organized labor, and generally announced his preference for one of the candidates for an important public office. But he held that bargaining sessions, not political rallies, would improve the lot of his Federation.

With the creation of the C.I.O. and the enactment of the Wagner Act in 1935 this Gompers policy radically changed. The C.I.O. was a manifestation of industrial, or vertical, unionism, quite unlike earlier craft unionism, which centered in the A.F.L. In its early years such leaders as Walter Reuther and Sidney Hillman were interested in political issues far more sweeping in scope than those immediately concerned with labor. The narrow interests of unions were not enough. Reuther, the son of a socialist, ultimately rose to the presidency of the C.I.O. He is a dedicated social, economic, and political reformer, his ideology not materially unlike what the British Labor Party leaders call "democratic socialism."

Reuther first penetrated the union headquarters of the new United Automobile Workers and rose to be its president. Then, with the personnel and money of that large and thriving union, it was only a step to take over domination of the Democratic Party in Michigan. Within a matter of a few years what had been a reliable Republican state was transformed into a relatively safe Democratic state, largely through the prodigious political efforts of the C.I.O. with bastions in Wayne County and Detroit and other industrial centers.

Other C.I.O. unions, following this example, were soon headed by political leaders and were projected into politics as allies of Democratic organizations in many other states. The C.I.O. Political Action Committee implemented the purposes of the leaders. With very, very few exceptions this apparatus openly identified itself with the fortunes of Democratic candidates.

With the merger of the A.F.L. and the C.I.O. came the most potent organization created by a minority in our history—the Committee on Political Education, in short, COPE. After the 1958 elections I carefully calculated the extent to which the unions' political action agencies, including COPE, had succeeded in influencing the election and thus the votes and actions of members of Congress. At least half of the members of the Senate as it stood in 1960 were substantial COPE supporters. And about 220 to 225 members of the House of Representatives, a slight majority, met the test of satisfying COPE's "voting-right" list. This brochure, entitled *How Your Senators and Representatives Voted, 1957–58*, had a distribution of millions of copies.

Labor influence in state elections has been equally important. In 1958 the AFL-CIO *News,* an official publication of the huge new federation, noted that it had backed seventeen of the twenty-three successful candidates for governor. The Republican Party was rocked by the loss of seven hundred seats in state legislatures in that same year. But that was only the bottom of a long decline. The Republican Party had lost one thousand seats in state legislatures from 1952 to 1956.

In the 1960 Presidential campaign, COPE worked prodigiously for the election of John F. Kennedy and for Democratic candidates for Congress. The Democratic successes of that year would not have been possible without the unsparing support given the Democratic Party by this minority auxiliary.

It is hardly an understatement to say that without the support of organized labor the Democratic Party would find itself in the minority.

Another powerful asset of the Democratic Party is the Negro minority. It is not as directly mobilized by any single organization as is labor under its monolithic union structure. But it has effective organizations working in its ranks. Negroes have become sufficiently conscious of their political power that in many if not most of the great cities they hold the margin for Democratic success. In the South the Negro vote is predominantly Democratic.

Majorities decide elections, but majorities have come to be dominated by active and skillfully directed minorities.

CHAPTER 13

News as an Instrument of Power

IMAGE-MAKING as an accessory of power politics originated neither on Madison Avenue nor on the Potomac.

Mother Nature did not put the hump on the back of Richard III. That was the creation of the hired scribblers of Henry VII in the years after the last of the Plantagenet kings fell fighting bravely on Bosworth Field. But Richard was no moral monster, nor would any grand jury on the evidence we now have indict him for the murder of the young princes.

Niccolò Machiavelli, an indefatigable, incorruptible public servant, wrote not what he was but what he saw of the corruption of his age, and has had a bad "press" down the centuries.

Pamphleteering of a political nature originated well before the Glorious Revolution of 1788–89 which placed William and Mary on the throne of England. But in the rise of parliamentary and party government, the pamphlet and then the press became an instrument of representative government. This was inevitable, since a party in power required not only the support of a parliamentary majority but public support or acquiescence. Patronage cared for majority support in Parliament, and patronage was used to assure the support of those with the means and genius to activate opinion elsewhere. The pamphlet, as it came to be regular in periodical appearance and name, was the beginning of what after many years earned the title "a free press." But in those years of the eighteenth century it was anything but free.

Sir Robert Walpole, Prime Minister from 1721 to 1742, developed to a fine art the capacity to manage not only Parliament but the early forerunners of the press. He devised means to cajole, bribe, or intimidate those who wrote for the public. When Walpole fell from power it was shown by a Committee of Secrecy that in ten years £50,000 of secret service money had been spent on pamphleteers and Treasury newspapers. Even his illustrious successor, the elder Pitt, found it necessary to subsidize several newspapers as well as theatrical producers, publishers, and booksellers. Later, at the time of the French Revolution, nine of Britain's most respected newspapers were on a regular annual allowance. Official advertising was also used copiously to influence those who disseminated news. The rise of the free press did not begin until the start of the nineteenth century.

I have had an exceptional opportunity to observe the making and dissemination of news and opinion in the United States over the past thirty years—for a time from a front seat in the Federal government, then from the status of a journalist. Of many developments and refinements, the following stand out:

1.   An astonishing growth in news media has taken place, with radio and television joining the newspaper and magazine.

2.   There has been an immense rise in the size of the Washington press corps. The Presidential press conference, which must be held in a commodious auditorium, is a visual reminder of change since Harding, Hoover, and Roosevelt held intimate office conferences.

3.   After the Wilson Administration, there appeared departmental press officers whose concern was to channel news to representatives of the privately controlled press. In Roosevelt's first years, the number of these greatly increased. For there were many newsmen in those depression years looking for government jobs. Now their number is legion, and their function is ostensibly

to provide a broad highway to the business of their agencies. In reality, these "public information," or "public relations," people are inclined to provide information favorable to the agency and the Administration in power. They prepare and hand out glowing press releases. Thus, many of them are far from helpers for the industrious, old-fashioned digging reporter. Rather, they frequently frustrate in one way or another an independent scrutiny of public business. The importance of these contact people in departments, bureaus, and agencies is enhanced by the growth of government with its vast bureaucracy and its increasingly complex activities. To a large extent, the average news-gatherer must either become a specialist in one or another activity or depend upon handouts and public relations people. The individual reporter may wander aimlessly through the corridors of a bureaucratic labyrinth. It is easier, in many cases more agreeable to his home office, to accept the sheaves of handouts, select, and rewrite rather than to scratch for original stories and news.

4. The deficiency in what the citizen is able to learn about his government is accentuated by the deplorable lack of equipment in a large part of the press corps. Reporters on newspapers yearn to achieve the distinction of a Washington assignment. Most of those selected are of above-average intelligence and ability, equipped with a good education. But the reporter is faced by the complexities of government operations or of Congressional activities. General knowledge and a "nose for news" is not enough. The tendency of many is to skim off the most superficial and most sensational. Digging, which requires study and inquiry and a strong mental back, is the habit of too few.

5. In the cold war, when security measures are important, an Administration has a fine, patriotic screen to frustrate criticism. Access can be denied to information on security grounds. The thwarted reporter cannot judge the validity of a prohibition because he cannot know the nature of the information. This is

especially true in the massive Departments of Defense and State. But all departments use a degree of censorship, and thousands of documents are stamped as classified or "for official eyes only."

6. Foremost among the providers of information is the White House press secretary. The first of these whom I knew was Stephen Early, who served under Roosevelt after 1933. He conceived it his responsibility to act as a buffer and at times a mediator between the President and the press corps. His loyalty to the President was unquestioned, but his loyalty to the press was equally pronounced. Many times he quietly suppressed some outbreak of the President toward what FDR was accustomed to call "unfairness" in news stories. Early never assumed the responsibility of becoming a White House spokesman. But in the Eisenhower years Jim Hagerty gave official policy statements in the name of the President. In the Kennedy regime Pierre Salinger not only presents news as a spokesman but is actually used in international diplomacy.

7. There is also the social life in Washington into which too many newsmen are lured and immersed. A bewildering number of dinners, cocktail parties, and other events offer contacts with people prominent in public office. Entanglements are created which may limit vision, dwarf judgment, and shake loyalty to that public interest to which journalists should be dedicated. This applies as well to an increased number of columnists who enjoy a circulation in many newspapers and nominally have a free hand to write independent opinions with news.

8. The White House is an awesome place, full of the reminders of a nation's history. The opportunity for a President and his entourage to invite influential people there and brief them is a powerful one. Few can resist the influence of such entertainment. Hence, many are subtly given "the treatment." If they have been critical, the edge of their attack is dulled. Often they come forth with new opinions and friendliness for the Administration. In the

Coolidge Administration a caustic, byline journalist was invited to one of the President's heavy New England breakfasts. His criticism ceased. A witty Senator remarked, "That's the first time I ever knew of a case in which ham and eggs went to a man's head."

Today, in managing the press, White House entertainment and invitations are continuous and effective. Publishers and top editors are ushered in and flattered. Frequently the effect of this flows down to employees. Whatever is published and is favorable to the regime is a source of power. Columnists and free-lance writers are treated with scrupulous attention. Flattery, entertainment, and access to invaluable sources, even if all this involves elaborate measures of travel and time by the President or members of his closest group, are frequently offered. A Presidential comment on an author's product may make it a best-seller.

The members of the working press are carefully managed. One correspondent says, "Today one newsman is given an exclusive story, yesterday it was another, tomorrow there will be another, and so on. A warm feeling goes far and wide and is stimulated either by memory of favors past or hopes of favors to come." To be critical or even to work for a critical newspaper is to court exclusion.

9. Newspapers and magazines pay high prices for a continuous stream of effusions, mostly ghosted, of those in high office. A conscientious public official spurns such emoluments. Once when Vice President Garner was offered five thousand dollars for a magazine article signed by him, he answered, "An article by John Garner is not worth that much. And the Vice Presidency is not for sale." But such consummate propriety is not always exercised. On one occasion Harry Hopkins made a diplomatic trip to Russia. On his return he declined to inform the press of his impressions. Then he wrote of the trip in a magazine article for which he received a large fee.

10. Any President is in a position to dominate the news. Theodore Roosevelt vigorously exploited this facet of the office, and he has been emulated by those having the desire and capacity to use this exalted position. Some news magazines and daily papers regularly devote special first-section attention to Presidential doings, however trivial. If news unfavorable to a President, his party, or his colleagues is about to appear he can often crowd it off the front page with some new action or statement or proposal. The opposition party may be scheduled to have a meeting which deserves publicity, but a President may destroy its prominence by some sort of news centered upon him.

11. President Kennedy is passionately concerned with his "image," immensely sensitive to public opinion. He winces at criticism and uses decisive means to meet it. He is, as has been assiduously publicized, interested in literature and in history. He cherishes the impression of an intellectual while he exercises the political sophistication of a machine boss. An editor recently said, "When a piece of news unfavorable to the Administration arises from some blunder or other action, the procedure is first to cover up, then to fog up, and then to counter with some sort of denial." Word went out to the Administration's contact people early in this regime: "Don't forget to give 'the Boss' credit and see that publicity should always be favorable to the 'team.' " This procedure was at first not fully carried out. The following is an excerpt from a Commerce Department memo which incorporates the word circulated in all departments:

At a White House meeting we have been advised again that speeches of Cabinet and sub-Cabinet officers do not contain sufficient reference to the President. It is to be kept in mind that, in announcing local projects, the President should be given a credit line in the lead paragraph.

"Incorrect," said Pierre Salinger. But the story was later confirmed.

As Walter Bagehot said of the passionate British public interest in the monarchy:

A *family* on the throne is an interesting idea also. It brings down the pride of sovereignty to the level of petty life. No feeling could seem more childish than the enthusiasm of the English at the marriage of the Prince of Wales. . . . The women—one half the human race at least—care fifty times more for a marriage than a ministry. . . . A princely marriage is the brilliant edition of a universal fact, and as such, it rivets mankind. We smile at the *Court Circular;* but remember how many people read the *Court Circular!* Its use is not in what it says, but in those to whom it speaks . . . a royal family sweetens politics by the seasonable addition of nice and pretty events. It introduces irrelevant facts into the business of government, but they are facts which speak to "men's bosoms" and employ their thoughts.

To state the matter shortly, Royalty is a government in which the attention of the nation is concentrated on one person doing interesting actions. A Republic is a government in which that attention is divided between many, who are all doing uninteresting actions.

Never before has a family with a member in the White House been so large, so physically attractive, so keenly sophisticated in politics. The Kennedys give the impression of dazzling motion, of achievement, and of doing those little things which are understood by everybody.

A great many of the Washington press corps are emotionally and ideologically outspoken supporters of Kennedy. They traveled with the candidates in 1960, and some profaned their profession by slanting their news dispatches against Nixon and for Kennedy. They committed sins of omission and commission. One reporter who had cast an absentee ballot for Kennedy could only deplore the attitude of many of his colleagues toward the Vice President: "I figure every guy deserves a fair shake." But bias blared in hundreds of leads.

The travels of the President and the members of his family are given tireless attention, and this is now bolstered by government facilities. Events such as Mrs. Kennedy's visits in India and Pakistan and her television tour of the White House captured immense audiences. These appearances are grist for the political mill. The U.S. Embassy in Ottawa gave suggested descriptions to Canadian reporters for a Kennedy visit. The President is "a glamorous political figure"; Mrs. Kennedy, "totally different from any traditional image of the President's wife"; Pierre Salinger, "a dynamo who resembles tireless competence in motion—a jaunty chunk of a man whose affable manner covers a steel-trap mind—precocious since childhood, Salinger is accustomed to outdistancing his contemporaries."

The interesting and commendable items in the Kennedys' private lives are carefully published. In every Kennedy campaign the great advantage of large means and numbers of attractive and ingratiating personalities was exercised. Once in power, this process has continued.

TR with his exploits, his riding and walking and hunting, set the pattern of stimulating interest by nonpolitical items. He advised his countrymen on methods of eating, playing, and reading. The Presidency became a high-placed pulpit for all sorts of preaching.

But compared with what is happening now, these exercises of TR and his family were minor distractions. The Kennedy regime works over the great engine of publicity with the attentiveness, skill, and tuning tools of a Mercedes-Benz racing crew. If an embarrassing situation arises in Washington because of an adverse vote in Congress or an Administration blunder, a Kennedy pops up in some other part of the world and commands the attention of the press. Frequently, rather than give out a direct statement, the President or an aide can "float" an idea, opinion, or plan through a newsman who is willing to relate the story by saying what the President "feels" or "thinks." The newsman becomes a sounding board or messenger, while the official family remains aloof, in a position to take credit, deny, or claim misinterpretation for the "feeling" or "thought."

While many whose business is informing the public shun flattery and favor and protest attempts to exploit their high calling, others go along. The Administration's process of publicity goes on incessantly, sometimes ruthlessly but always effectively, as a means of consolidating power.

CHAPTER 14

Welfare Unlimited, I

ONE day in early 1936 Harry Hopkins had lunch with me in my apartment in New York. He had been head of three relief agencies which had succeeded each other in the years since 1933. At that moment his operation was the Works Progress Administration, which was created in 1935. Because President Roosevelt liked the Hopkins habit of spending rapidly, he had transferred a great deal of money to WPA from Secretary Ickes' slow-moving Public Works Administration. And the disposition of these funds was subject largely to the discretion of Hopkins.

I had known Hopkins well since his earlier assignment as relief administrator in New York in 1932, and he ruminated at length that day about his career as a social worker in earlier years, his concepts of government service, his social and political philosophy, and the immediate decision which at that moment was uppermost in his mind.

In his distribution of Federal relief money he had for nearly three years ignored political considerations. But now, he said, the heavy pressure was building up from the various urban machines to loosen the strings in a political year. He was not enamored of the bosses or their methods. But he said he had finally decided that they would provide useful instruments in getting votes in large masses for what he regarded as a great crusade, an experiment in government of which Roosevelt was the leader and the inspiration. Thus he squared his early idealism with this new cause. And he said he had decided to open wide the Federal purse. Thus was consummated the immensely fruitful marriage of welfare and politics in the United States. The record shows that welfare outlays reached new peaks in 1936, 1938, and 1940—all election years.

It is true, as I have shown in an earlier chapter, that political consideration is not the sole motive in the immense growth of Federal welfare. Present-day liberalism, so far as welfare is concerned, has many components—the drying up of philanthropic sources by heavy taxes, the impoverishment of the states and local communities because of Federal invasion of their tax sources, the belief of so many people that to concentrate welfare activities in a central government might be more efficient, and a genuine humanitarian instinct which seeks happiness and plenty for everyone. There has been the growth of powerful minority blocs, which increase by what they feed upon. Immense Federal welfare programs can be achieved through a political government.

For the purpose of showing how the Federal welfare activities have grown since the relatively small beginnings at the time Hopkins made his decision, I asked Miss Emily Hammond, a remarkably competent student of the many welfare activities of government, to prepare the significant data. Her statistical tabulations were compiled from the various Presidential budget reports and other official documents. To cite the authority for each of them would unduly lengthen this chapter. But they are all incorporated in the report which Miss Hammond submitted to me. Her explanation of the data is this:

"Welfare" in the sense of personal aid and as used in these tables includes most, but not all, of the Federal programs defined as welfare on pages 990 and 991 of the Budget for 1962—under the headings "public assistance," "promotion of public health," "promotion of education," and "other welfare services." It also includes veterans' services and benefits, and Federal aids to housing, with the exception of the Federal Home Loan Bank Board and the Farmers Home Administration. Most important of all, it includes the "social insurances" which do not appear in the budgets proper at all but were sanctioned by the Supreme Court as welfare, not insurance. Some will certainly question my inclusion of unemployment compensation as a Federal program, because the states administer it and tax employers to pay benefits. However, it was the Social Security Act of 1935 that forced the states to collect these taxes, and the money collected has to be deposited in the Unemployment Trust Fund in the U. S. Treasury before the state agencies may use it. The states in this case are in effect the Treasury's tax collectors and administrators. Control is in the Federal government. No attempt has been made to be all-inclusive of welfare programs. These tables therefore represent an understatement of the immensity of the Federal activities in welfare.

In the fiscal year which ended while Congress was enacting the first Social Security Act, Federal welfare payments were these:

TABLE A

SELECTED FEDERAL WELFARE AND SERVICE
PROGRAMS' EXPENDITURES, FISCAL 1935
(In thousands of dollars)

Recovery and Relief	2,846,082
Civilian Conservation Corps	435,509
Veterans	605,573
Housing	27,874
Vocational Rehabilitation	1,100
Education	14,542
Public Health	12,945
Maternal and Child Welfare	342
Total:	3,943,967

Before coming to an explanation of the history and the nature of various Federal welfare programs, it will be useful to show the growth of such programs measured in dollars.

For comparison with the programs and costs in 1935, the following table shows 1960:

TABLE B

SELECTED FEDERAL WELFARE AND SERVICE
PROGRAMS' EXPENDITURES, FISCAL 1960
(In thousands of dollars)

Veterans	5,059,667
Housing	309,065
Special Milk Program	81,181
School Lunch Program	152,832
Vocational Rehabilitation	61,303
Education	459,038
Public Health	743,711
Public Assistance	2,061,453
Maternal and Child Welfare	49,658
"Social Insurance"	
Old-Age and Survivor Insurance	10,269,700
Disability Insurance	528,300
Railroad Retirement	916,400
Unemployment Compensation	2,699,225
Total:	23,391,533

Thus the welfare activities which are listed have risen in cost from $3,943,967,000 to $23,391,533,000. That is 493 per cent. The increase in population over that period was 42 per cent.

The table on page 94 shows the steady growth of welfare as indicated by costs in 1945, 1955, and 1960.

The years indicated here were marred only by temporary recessions. In general, they were years of marked prosperity and well-being.

The growth continues year by year, as is shown by a comparison of 1960 with 1961.[1]

---

[1] Since this is written before the close of the fiscal year 1962 and the Budget estimates do not correspond with the categories used in the following tables, it would not be helpful to bring the story up to this date of publication. But there is every evidence that in fiscal 1962, the first full year of the Kennedy Administration, there will be startling increases all along the line.

TABLE C

SELECTED FEDERAL WELFARE AND SERVICE PROGRAMS' EXPENDITURES, FISCAL 1945, 1955, AND 1960
(In thousands of dollars)

	1945	1955	1960
Veterans	2,093,586	4,456,963	5,059,667
Housing	118,250	153,190	309,065
Special Milk Program			81,181
School Lunch Program		83,099	152,832
Vocational Rehabilitation	7,543	26,919	61,303
Education	73,069	260,798	459,038
Public Health	131,100	251,980	743,711
Public Assistance	402,229	1,428,058	2,061,453
Maternal and Child Welfare	56,714	30,833	49,658
"Social Insurance"			
Old-Age and Survivor Insurance	267,000	4,333,100	10,269,700
Disability Insurance			528,300
Railroad Retirement	141,000	569,300	916,400
Unemployment Compensation	71,937	2,087,944	2,699,225
Total:	3,362,428	13,682,184	23,391,533

TABLE D

SELECTED FEDERAL WELFARE AND SERVICE PROGRAMS' EXPENDITURES, FISCAL 1960 AND 1961
(In thousands of dollars)

	1960	1961
Veterans	5,059,667	5,410,321
Housing	309,065	501,890
Special Milk Program	81,181	87,000
School Lunch Program	152,832	154,359
Vocational Rehabilitation	61,303	70,490
Education	459,038	499,146
Public Health	743,711	856,286
Public Assistance	2,061,453	2,169,813
Maternal and Child Welfare	49,658	54,143
"Social Insurance"		
Old-Age and Survivor Insurance	10,269,700	11,184,500
Disability Insurance	528,300	704,000
Railroad Retirement	916,400	981,800
Unemployment Compensation	2,699,225	4,124,908
Total:	23,391,533	26,798,656

The expression "general welfare" appears twice in the Constitution. In the Preamble it has no legal significance, but in Article I, Section 8, Congress is authorized to levy taxes "to provide for the common defense and general welfare." It can be argued that the intended meaning of "general" in this language means the collective welfare and not the sum of many welfares. Since the Supreme Court has held otherwise, however, the constitutional issue is closed. But in so holding, the Court opened the dykes for an immense flood of Federal costs with which we are now contending.

In the years since the 1930's Congress and various administrations have in the name of welfare not only added to the burdens of the present but have mortgaged the future. Program has been added to program—most of them morally if not legally imposing an obligation on succeeding Congresses to continue increasingly large appropriations, with little practical means of revising or discontinuing them.

An accounting of recipients of Federal aid and assistance—including not only those under social security but veterans' benefits, unemployment compensation, and many other programs—would be an almost impossible task. For in some categories the numbers change from month to month and from day to day. Moreover, there are a great many who are receiving more than one kind of assistance. But it is possible to show those who are recipients under the major programs of what is called social security:

TABLE E

SOCIAL SECURITY RECIPIENTS
JUNE 1961

Program

Old-Age, Survivors, and Disability Insurance	15,624,182
Old-Age Assistance	2,296,190
Aid to Dependent Children	3,382,865
Aid to the Blind	105,608
Aid to the Permanently and Totally Disabled	383,952
Total:	21,792,797

CHAPTER 15

Welfare Unlimited, II

A VERY long library shelf, reinforced, might hold up under the weight of a critical examination of Federal interests in welfare. Here it is necessary to summarize briefly the status of a few of these programs. As the preceding tabulations show, these programs are proliferating. Unless this phase of our government's activities is rationalized, reconsidered, and in most cases reorganized, the burden on the budget will be so heavy that any party in power will be forced to curtail other responsibilities of government, even at the expense of national security. This has happened in Britain, even under the Conservative restoration.

Old-Age, Survivors, and Disability Insurance (OASDI)

In 1937 the Supreme Court declared the Federal old-age benefits under the law of 1935 to be constitutional under the general welfare clause. The Justice Department in its defense of the Act had pleaded, "not to be said to constitute a plan for insurance." Before World War II the maximum monthly benefits were $45.60, with family benefits up to $85. In 1958 these sums were fixed at $127 and $254. In 1956 disability benefits were initiated, and in 1958 dependents of disabled workers were provided for.

In 1956 the retirement age for women was fixed at sixty-two. Men were to begin their benefits at sixty-five in the early years. Now the age is sixty-two for them also.

Altogether, there have been fifty extensions of the benefits since 1950. At the beginning, employers and employees each were taxed 1 per cent on wages up to $3,000. In 1950 the rate was increased to a total of 3 per cent on wages up to $3,600. In 1954 there was another increase, this time to 4 per cent on wages up to $4,200. In 1958 the rate went to 5 per cent on wages up to $4,800. Now the total rate is 6¼ per cent, but it will automatically increase to 7¼ per cent, until 1966 when it will go to 8¼ per cent. Then, in 1968, it will be 9¼ per cent.

That the system has become an instrument of politics is illustrated by the fact that regularly in recent years the broadening of the coverage has been made in election years. Indeed, in the past five years the fund has been rapidly depleted. Some people are paying more social security taxes than their regular income levies. And the probabilities are that there will be perversions of the system for a long time to come unless the entire contraption is utterly reorganized.

Public Assistance

When the Social Security Act was in preparation, it was recognized that many people approaching sixty-five would either not be covered or would not work long enough to meet eligibility requirements for Federal old-age benefits. Hence, "Old-Age Assistance" was set up. It was hoped that this would be temporary, since equities of those "insured" had more time to rise before retirement. But Old-Age Assistance has increased immensely.

The general term "public assistance" covers a large number of the progeny of the original Social Security Act. There are programs of Federal grants-in-aid to the states for Old-Age Assistance, Aid to Dependent Children, Aid to the Blind, Aid to the Permanently and Totally Disabled, Vendor Payments for Medical Care for Recipients of Public Assistance, and Medical Assistance for the Aged. These do not include the Maternal and Child Welfare program or the Public Health provisions of the Social Security Act, which are administered separately by the Department of Health, Education and Welfare, nor the wholly state-financed assistance programs, which are called "general assistance."

All public assistance programs are administered by the states, or states and local governments, according to Federal rules and regulations. The states must have Federally approved plans in order to qualify for Federal financial aid. All public assistance recipients must be in need, with the exception of the aged receiving medical assistance under the 1960 program, who are eligible if they are "in need" or "near need."

Although state plans must be uniform within the state, the states differ widely in their interpretation of need, in property allowances, relative-responsibility laws, and lien and recovery laws. Studies show that in states with comparatively strict relative-responsibility laws and lien and recovery laws, case loads run lighter than in the more liberally inclined states.

In spite of the great increase in the number of persons receiving OASDI benefits, more and more Americans are recipients of public assistance. The easy money has been an open invitation to chiselers.

Uncle Sam, M.D.

Without attempting to evaluate every program already in operation, let us review the already towering Federal medical-health appropriations and payments to persons because of disability, financed entirely or in part by the Federal government. Twenty Federal departments, agencies, and commissions had medical-health budgets totaling more than $4 billion in 1962. Budgets of the big three—the Department of Health, Education and Welfare, the Veterans Administration, and the Department of Defense—came to $2 billion, $1.1 billion, and $848 million respectively. All twenty departments had medical-health budgets totaling $4,437,746,072. Add to this, payments to individuals because of disability amounting to $5 billion, and we see that the Federal government is already in the health picture to a thumping amount of more than $9.5 billion.

Some programs are sound and fall logically within the realm of Federal authority. Others, which might well reside with state and local authorities, have come within Federal jurisdiction because, with Federal absorption of tax sources, the states, counties, and communities cannot bear the expense of these projects alone.

The Department of HEW has its division of Hospital Facilities, its National Institutes of Health (dealing with many matters from research and training to the construction of waste-treatment plants), its community health activities, its environmental health activities, and many other bureaus and programs.

The Veterans Administration budget is directed largely toward the VA hospitals, while the Department of Defense devotes its medical budget to service hospitals and the care of servicemen and their families.

The Kerr-Mills bill, passed in 1960, has now been implemented in several states and is tied to the states' medical-assistance-for-the-aged plans. This program can meet the financing of all health services of those over sixty-five who are unable to do so. The states have an obligation to implement it effectively.

The King-Anderson plan of 1962 is a long step in a long and probably endless road. While piously stating that control of hospitals and doctors is not involved, the plan contains elaborate provisions for supervision and for making of specifications by the Secretary of HEW. If this does not involve control, we may say that Bismarck's hand was feeble, that a Marine drill sergeant has no control or authority over recruits.

The liberals' intent in the medical-health area is clear. Speaking of his defunct bill, former Representative Aimé Forand remarked, "If we can only break through and get our foot inside the door, then we can expand the program after that." Walter Reuther came to the point and expressed the position of many liberal labor leaders: "It is no secret that the UAW is officially on record as backing a program of national health insurance . . ."

On a dark, rainy night in February, 1950, in Bristol, England, I had a most interesting evening with the Socialist firebrand, Aneurin Bevan, Minister of Health, in charge of the new National Health Service. The political meeting which we attended was a very rowdy affair. A tough dock worker engaged the sturdy Bevan in a running fire of mutual recrimination. At one point the heckler drew from his mouth a plate of false teeth and waved it at Bevan, who shouted, "I am the Minister of Health and I am going to take those teeth away from you." The man shouted back, "I paid five pounds for these and they are my own." The argument ceased, and Bevan put on as forceful a demonstration of crowd control and incitement as any demagogue I have been privileged to hear.

After the meeting, two other American newspapermen, Bevan, and I spent three hours discussing issues in a restaurant. I best remember his reply to my question about how he intended to get control of the British medical profession: "We have got the hospitals, and that means we will control the doctors. They can't practice without places to practice."

"Government control" is preferable to "socialism" in describing Britain's National Health Service. Though popular, it has sandwiched a great slab of bureaucracy between patients and the doctors which even those who support the system admit and deplore. The Health Service's costs by July, 1961, were five times the original estimate. "If only we could eliminate the bumbling officials," one supporter remarks. In the United States such a system would entail a bureaucracy of far greater dimensions. But it is precisely this Federal control that liberals seek "by gradual means."

The Federal Role in Housing

Federal aid to housing, which started so modestly in World War I and expired after the emergency, reappeared in various forms during the depression and World War II, boomed in the prosperous 1950's, and now is a profligate multibillion-dollar Federal enterprise.

The Housing and Home Finance Agency is parent organization to the Federal National Mortgage Association, which engages in secondary market operations. The Federal Housing Administration and the Public Housing Administration insure long-term loans for building, purchase, or repair of commercial construction, multifamily dwellings, and single-family private houses. The Public Housing Administration promotes low-rent public housing for the low, but not the lowest, income groups.

The Housing and Home Finance Agency itself engages in giving or lending Federal funds for college housing, public facilities, public works planning, urban planning, slum clearance, and urban renewal, community disposal operations, housing for the elderly, and farm housing research.

In 1955, a Hoover Commission task force warned:

> The Housing Act of 1954 could mark the beginning of one of the most significant shifts in governmental viewpoint ever accepted by the Congress of the United States. The man who heads the H.H.F.A. . . . must concern himself, as a manager, with the entire problem of planning the nation's cities on a national basis . . .
> The task force is apprehensive over the trend of these developments which threaten to reduce further and further the fields in which individual American citizens will have the responsibility for and influence over the conduct of their personal and home-town affairs. It is true that the new programs are optional and no State or city need participate if its people do not want it to. But those who want the benefits must conform to the plans, and the national tax burden falls alike on those who participate and those who decline.

The Housing Act of 1961 goes much further, violating sound principles of welfare by providing aid for home ownership and rental housing to moderate-income families. Among many other liberalizations, it provides additional aid to small towns, to business firms displaced by urban renewal, to rehabilitation housing, college housing, nursing homes, and public works planning. A transit program to help cities and towns overcome their commuting problems, and another program to help state and local government acquire land for parks, recreation areas, "and other permanent open space use" further centralize responsibility in bureaucratic hands. Also, there is now no limit to the FHA's authority to insure loans, although a cutoff date, 1965, was provided. Senator Harry F. Byrd estimated in 1961 that Federal aid to housing had amounted to $115 billion.

This great adventure in Federal housing has had the following consequences:

1.   HHFA and its subordinate agencies constitute an engine of inflation and deflation beyond the reach of the control of the Federal Reserve System.

2.   In effect, the Federal government is subsidizing obsolescence. It is building the slums of twenty-five years hence.

3.   The method of financing the bulk of Federal aid to housing is through the "back door" practice of drawing money from the Treasury, thus bypassing the Congressional appropriations committees. The 1961 Housing Act provided an outlay from the government of only $343 million, but the total authorizations amounted to almost $5 billion. The future is thus heavily mortgaged.

4.   It is most doubtful whether, under Federal rules and regulations, public housing really helps the most needy. It provides a haven for the investments of the rich by tax exemption of an immense amount of federally insured local public-housing bonds.

5.   Urban renewal puts a premium on the violation of private property rights by offering Federal funds to cities and towns if they will exercise their power of eminent domain, thus ousting and scattering well-established communities. It provides a tremendous opportunity for profits to speculators who buy cheaply into slum

areas and then sell the unimproved land back to the governments concerned at excessively inflated prices.

Unemployment Compensation

The Federal-state program of Unemployment Compensation was initiated in the Social Security Act of 1935, which established the Unemployment Trust Fund and empowered the Social Security Board to approve or disapprove and annually to pass on state unemployment compensation laws according to certain criteria.

In order to induce the states to set up their own unemployment compensation systems in accordance with these statutory standards, the Act authorized the levy of a Federal excise tax on all employers of eight or more employees, beginning at 1 per cent and rising in three years to 3 per cent of the first $3,000 of each employee's wages. However, against this tax employers could take up to 90 per cent credit for contributions to a state unemployment compensation plan approved by the Board.

In due course all states responded to the threat of the Federal taxing power and passed laws of their own which were approved by the Social Security Board. As a result, the Treasury has until recently collected only .3 per cent of taxable wages and paid them into the Treasury's general fund.

The Federal government also makes appropriations for a fund to pay the expenses of the Federal supervision of the system in the states and also to pay the states for their administrative costs. This fastens Federal control more firmly on the states, since if at any time the Federal authority fails to approve a state system, there can be withheld money for the state's administrative expenses as well as funds for benefit payments.

Thus, the Federal government exercises a wide margin of discretion and control of the state systems. But even this is not enough to satisfy liberal labor leaders and liberals in Congress. The drive is for a federalization of the whole system.

States have developed unemployment compensation systems

which vary widely in methods of financing, waiting periods, disqualifications, duration of benefits, and benefit amounts. All have grown. Today, the average unemployment compensation weekly benefit is worth 44 per cent more in purchasing power than in 1939.

An evil which has entered the system generally is the refusal of unemployed workers to accept jobs and the disposition to cling to the unemployment benefits.

There can be no objection to an unemployment compensation system which will provide aid by taxes levied on industry to tide over workers who are involuntarily separated from their means of earning a living. But with the abuses which have developed and the constant pressure to liberalize payments, there develops what is in essence a subsidy for unemployment.

This is a remarkable contradiction in the policies of liberalism. On the one hand it moves to create unemployment, and on the other it preaches greater economic growth and "full employment." But by the burden on production which the present excesses in the system impose, the means for more production are severely curtailed.

Veterans

From the beginning, Federal aid to veterans and their dependents on the one hand has been defended as the mere extension of reward for patriotic service rendered a grateful country. On the other hand, it has been damned as a political football and a "billion-dollar boondoggle." Something of the truth exists in both estimations.

Certainly, the widows and orphans of men who have lost their lives in our wars should have the best the rest of us can rightfully give them. Also, veterans with service-connected disabilities deserve compensation.

The G.I. Bill of Rights provided college education for thousands of young Americans who might not otherwise have had it, and unemployment benefits for thousands more who could not find jobs upon returning to civilian life. For still other thousands it offered the chance to chisel and bring disrepute to the whole program.

The Veterans Administration's vast welfare operations based on need are a perfectly legitimate Federal function. Furthermore, the income supplement system now in use should prove a valuable guide in the reform of other welfare programs.

CHAPTER 16

Fiscal Delusions and Deceptions

SINCE massive amounts of money are necessary to sustain the superstate, great ingenuity is essential to exact the utmost from the taxpayer. No citizen likes to be taxed, but there is no limit to the capacity of clever people to befuddle and confuse him.

The politician who is intent upon his trade of giving lavishly while exacting the wherewithal painlessly has found an invaluable ally in recent years to be the practitioner of the "dismal science" of economics. No science has been capable of creating so much confusion by a lavish use of mathematics and semantic tricks. There have been and are many economists who are realistic and dedicated disciples of truth, but many others arrive at dubious conclusions by the use of statistical tricks. Their researches teem with facts. But many of them follow the rule of Mark Twain: "First get your facts. And then you may distort them as much as you wish." Because economists are so useful to the practical art of politics, the Washington bureaucracy is well supplied with them.

Closely related to the multitude of economists in the operations of government are the statisticians. They, too, play a major part in mulcting the taxpayer while they blind him with rows of figures.

In the years during which Eisenhower was President and Congress was dominated by Democrats, the President's Council of

Economic Advisers and the majority of the Joint Congressional Committee on the Economic Report, by the use of the same collections of statistics, were able to arrive at wholly contradictory conclusions about the status of the economy and what should be done about it.

Another choice proof of this contention is the wizardry practiced by the experts in the Bureau of Reclamation of the Department of the Interior. Reclamation and power projects that in the light of common sense are wasteful and unnecessary are proposed and passed by Congress. But, by tricks with the components of cost and interest and what are called benefit-cost ratios, we are led to believe that these are sound and productive investments.

To attribute all of the fiscal make-believe which goes on in the economic calculations of our Federal government to the great vogue of Keynesian economics is utterly unfair to the ingenuity of Americans who have contrived new applications of the teachings of the famous British economist.

The nature of the congenial marriage of politics and economics is portrayed by three notable examples.

Spending Without Control

The wise men who wrote the Constitution, vividly aware of the bitter struggles between extravagant kings and Parliaments over the control of the purse, gave to Congress, not the President, certain means of maintaining fiscal responsibility. Those were the powers to levy taxes for Constitutional purposes and to "borrow money on the credit of the United States." As Congress implemented these powers, there emerged a responsible system which was maintained for a long time by tradition, habit, and Congressional prudence. The House Ways and Means Committee handled not only taxes but expenditures, and its actions were subject to action by the respective houses and, in case of differences, by compromise in conference committees. The consolidation of taxing and spending in the same committee of origin made it possible to balance outgo with income.

In 1865, however, a separate Appropriations Committee was created. The Senate likewise created its Committee on Appropriations to work alongside its Finance Committee. Thus there began a process of decentralized control which in our time amounts to practically no control at all.

In the 1880's various committees came to be responsible for appropriations in their respective areas of interest.

In 1921 major reforms were enacted in the Budget and Accounting Act. This made the two appropriations committees responsible for all appropriations. But to tighten the procedure still more, Congress created in 1946 a Joint Committee on the Legislative Budget to consider both outgo and income. This provision, however, has become a dead letter. The 1921 Act also set up the Presidential Budget and the General Accounting Office under a Comptroller General responsible to Congress.

Various committees still make "authorizations" which are really no more than "hunting licenses for appropriations."

But in the past forty years the expenditures have burgeoned into so many fields and in such amounts that real control has been lost.

The largest proportion of money spent which is not subject to annual survey and appropriation by the appropriations committees is in what are called carry-over funds. These are (1) one-year appropriations which if obligated that year may run into two more years; (2) multiple-year appropriations open for spending for specified years more; (3) no-year appropriations running until the purpose is achieved; and (4) permanent appropriations, such as the interest on the public debt.

There are also certain fixed charges, such as contributions to trust funds.

Open-end programs are for such purposes as aid to agriculture, to the states in grants, and to veterans. It is said that these are necessary because the amounts cannot be calculated in advance. Then there is the greatest of all irregularities, which provides that certain executive agencies may borrow from the Treasury. This is called "back-door" spending. Finally, there are implied obligations for authorized programs, passed annually without reconsideration of the need and purpose. These are mainly for grants to states and aid to veterans.

It is estimated that at least two-thirds of Federal expenditures annually are in the foregoing annually uncontrollable items. Only one-third is relatively controllable annually by the appropriations committees.

Trust Funds

Various funds dedicated to supplying the money for specific services and benefits have been established and are known as trust funds. The most important of these is the Social Security Trust Fund. Income is collected by social security taxes and earmarked for social security payments. When there is an excess of collections over outgo, the money is invested in Federal securities. The government then spends the proceeds from such sales for its general purposes. When the fund needs money over its income from taxes, it sells the bonds back to the government.

Obviously, the values in the funds are merely the promises to pay by the Federal government. Little or no review is made by congressional committees because these funds are previously authorized expenditures. These are not really trust funds at all in the sense in which that term is used in private affairs. There is no check as to whether the income from the specified taxes is enough for the annual outlays. In the social security fund the outgo is already more than the income from social security taxes.

The highway program provides that the Federal government contribute 90 per cent to designated highways and the state 10 per cent. The efficiency and regularity of the immense highway system is now at least reviewed annually by responsible congressional committees. But many investigations have shown lack of wisdom and needless extravagance.

Back-Door Spending

The Constitution states that "No money shall be drawn from the Treasury but in consequence of appropriations made by law." By law and custom over a period of 143 years the letter of this provision was observed. Appropriations were an annual affair.

These restrictions, by Constitution and House rules, are still in effect. They follow a principle established in bitter conflicts in England between Parliament and the King. They mean that the Executive shall always be restricted by Congress' control of the purse strings.

The change that came about paid a dubious respect to the word "appropriations" by devising a means of exacting money from the Treasury which avoided the use of that term. A back door was opened through which billions have been drawn in the past thirty years.[1]

This violation of Constitutional and traditional procedure was inaugurated in the powers given to an institution which, during its life, was of inestimable value, the Reconstruction Finance Corporation. Under the act creating the RFC, the Treasury was told to lend money and finance such loans by selling Federal bonds to the public. No congressional appropriation was required. By 1957, when the RFC was finally abolished, the Treasury had advanced $26.6 billion and had received only $13.6 billion in repayment. Congress ordered the remainder written off.

The door thus opened has been used by many agencies, including the Commodity Credit Corporation, the Export-Import Bank, the Federal National Mortgage Association, the Home Owners Loan Corporation, the Federal Housing Administration, and

[1] The Treasury reports this in *Authorizations to Spend for Public Debt Transactions, 1932–61.*

others.[2] The back door has also been used to provide college housing and urban renewal loans, direct loans to veterans, defense production loans, subscriptions to the International Bank, and a loan to Britain. In 1961 President Kennedy proposed that an $8.8 billion bill for foreign aid be financed through the back door, but the plan was frustrated by Congress.

From the beginning in 1932 to midyear 1960, $114,489,000,-000 had gone through the back door. In the first session of the eighty-seventh Congress in 1961 there were, in bills passed or pending, $23.7 billion in such spending.

There is an infinite variety of operations encompassed in this method, but only one need be described here. This is the use of what is called a "revolving fund," allotted to an agency with authority to finance a continuing cycle of operations without any further action by Congress.

Thus Congress has deliberately, and in violation of the clear intent of the Constitution, relinquished its control over a large area of the fiscal operations of the government. It has been of little avail that responsible members and chairmen in the House have castigated this practice. Clarence Cannon, Chairman of the House Appropriations Committee, said on one occasion, "Let us vote down this conference report with this silly back-door shenanigan put in by the Senate. It is financial duplicity. It is fiscal insanity." But the practice continues and grows.

Without fiscal control there can be no control of government. In the President's budget submitted in January, 1962, there are presented many programs whose purposes seem fine to him, but little is presented as practical means for achieving them. As a Senator, John F. Kennedy argued on one occasion quite passionately for fiscal responsibility. This early crusade, however, was forgotten by him after his inauguration as President.

[2] The Rural Electrification Administration had the use of the back door until Congress removed it from the list of favored agencies. But in President Kennedy's recommendations for 1963 he asked that it be restored as a back-door agency.

CHAPTER 17

The Twin Destroyers

THE late Robert Hunter spent the final years of his life in a study of the forces and circumstances through which basic changes have taken place in the structure and patterns of society and government in history. He was concerned with the causes of revolutions.[1] He found that in notable revolutions there has been much the same cycle of forces. All ended in some form of dictatorship. In almost all, heavy confiscatory taxation, devaluation, and inflation played a major part. Hunter sums up these demoralizing economic forces under five heads, in the order of their appearance: heavy taxation, the abolition of debt, devaluation of the means of exchange, inflation, and outright confiscation.

The Blight of Excessive Taxation

In government, ancient and modern, the forces of spending always rise to meet income. This immutable truth is amusingly but accurately noted in Parkinson's Law.[2] Spending, however, stresses heavily the limits of income and, with progressive elevation of rates, a point is reached at which there are diminishing returns. In ancient times that point was regarded as about 10 per cent of income. When the burden reached that percentage,

[1] Revolution (New York: Harper and Brothers, 1940).
[2] C. Northcote Parkinson (Boston: Houghton Mifflin, 1957). Also, The Law and the Profits by the same author (Houghton Mifflin, 1960).

taxpayers migrated to another area where taxes were less excessive. In the *Book of Exodus* we learn that when the Jews found the exactions of the Egyptians unbearable, they decided that it was "time to study the atlas."

In our more complicated age economists have reckoned that the point of diminishing returns is higher—at about 25 per cent of the national income, according to John Maynard Keynes in 1923. As the rates on a considerable number of individuals and businesses moved higher and higher, certain forces were generated which were inflationary. This conclusion was confirmed by Colin Clark in 1945. Excessive taxation and inflation, therefore, interact and become accomplices in the same malignant processes of destroying economic productivity, personal security, and national morality.

Desirous beneficiaries of government largesse generate political power to meet their demands. Governments, to avoid the wrath of those who are required to pay, create more and more clever devices to hide the impact—hidden taxes, devious and deceptive reporting on fiscal transactions, plus confiscation of capital by inflation. Also, there are political forces which are powerful enough to secure various exemptions for privileged interests. The tax system is befogged by infinite complexities. Then there is a counterdrive directed by experts employed by taxpayers to avoid the impact of high taxes. Then government counterattacks with battalions of its own experts. This, of course, not only increases the costs of business and individual enterprise but enlarges the cost of the bureaucracy. But legal avoidance is not the whole story. Evasion and cheating grow in all brackets of taxpayers. And the ultimate result is general contempt for laws which are regarded as unfair, discriminatory, and oppressive. The final result is contempt for all law and government.

The United States has long since passed the critical 25 per cent level. The Tax Foundation estimated in December, 1961, that the total government spending—Federal, state, and local—would in the fiscal year 1962 rise to $173 billion. Tax receipts from those units of government would be $143 billion. The disparity would be accounted for by miscellaneous revenues and by deficit financing by the Federal government.

Since we are concerned here with Federal finances, the following table is one estimate of the expected Federal budget receipts in 1962 classified by sources:

FEDERAL BUDGET RECEIPTS
(Millions of Dollars)

	1962
Individual Income Taxes	50,200
Corporation Income Taxes	21,600
Excise Taxes	13,095
Employment Taxes	13,116
Estate and Gift Taxes	1,973
Customs	1,134
Miscellaneous Receipts	3,809
Total Gross Receipts	104,926
Deduct:	
Transfers to Trust Funds	16,404
Refunds of Receipts	5,522
Interfund Transactions	667
Total Net Budget Receipts	82,333

Since "employment taxes" are a combination of imposts upon employees and employers, they are really income taxes. Hence, of the expected receipts of the Federal government the total income taxes amount to 80 per cent. This enormous burden gives rise to a multitude of ill effects. A few examples must suffice here.

1. The complexity of the income tax laws, together with administrative regulations and judicial decisions, shrouds the subject with a cloud of obscurity hardly penetrable by those who collect or those who pay. General lack of public understanding and vast amounts of litigation result.

2. The high progressive rates on the upper and middle per-

sonal incomes discourage and forbid adequate investment and capital formation.

3. The heavy tax on corporations compels the use of indirect but perfectly legal devices to compensate employees and reward investors.

4. Since a corporation tax must be calculated as a cost of production, the effect is the creation of taxes on consumers, hidden in the price. Thus, the corporation tax is in its essentials an excise tax. There are, as the table above shows, additional excises, most of which are hidden from the consumer. The heavy corporation tax also restricts capital formation. Moreover, both the corporation tax and the individual income tax repress the incentive to establish new industries.

5. High and progressive taxation destroys the expenditure of that extra effort which is a key to progress. "Why," asks the individual, "should I take on this extra labor when the compensation I would receive would simply move me into a higher bracket where Uncle Sam will take a larger part of what I make?"

6. A high tax is the mother of debt. Millions of Americans seldom pay cash, even for their necessities. Vacations are paid for by future installments. Economists and businessmen have valid arguments for installment selling. But the accumulation of a massive amount of debt is essentially a danger to economic stability. I have never been convinced, even by my friends among our economists, that a major factor in the crash which accelerated the great depression of the 1930's was not debt accumulated by installment buying.

7. The excessive complications of the tax laws and regulations take the full-time talents of a large class of intelligent individuals who are productive only in the sense that their skills save the capital of those who employ them.

8. The same political forces which demand and get so much from the government have also created many loopholes, special privileges, and exemptions.

9. High and progressive taxation makes cheating the government a national pastime. Tax laws that are patently unjust breed violations; first, of those specific laws and, finally, of all laws.

The Blight of Inflation

In Harry Scherman's brilliant account of the bad faith which through the ages has characterized all governments' way with money matters, he tells of the ancient uses of paper money.[3] In an area in China a century before the birth of Christ, the people used as a medium of exchange one-foot-square pieces of the skin of white deer. The emperor, however, gathered all the white deer that could be found into his own park. Then he issued an order making it a criminal offense for any of his subjects to own white deer. Thus he obtained a monopoly of money.

Scherman refers to another incident, more than twenty centuries later. In the early days of the Administration of Franklin D. Roosevelt, the lawyers discovered an almost forgotten piece of legislation which was passed to meet emergencies in the First World War—the Trading with the Enemy Act. By executive order, all persons were to deliver all gold coins, gold certificates, and bullion to the Treasury in exchange for paper currency, and the banks were to deliver their gold to the Federal Reserve. Fines up to ten thousand dollars and jail terms were fixed for those who refused to obey. Roosevelt claimed as justification that Congress had authorized this action. Later, in January, 1934, Congress authorized the President to reduce the gold valuation of the dollar by 50 per cent if he deemed it necessary. And then by executive order the President reduced the gold value of a dollar almost by half by the device of raising the price of gold, all of which, under the earlier action, belonged to the government, to thirty-five dollars an ounce.

The difference in time was two thousand years. This was a

[3] *The Promises Men Live By* (New York: Random House, 1938), Chapter XVII.

President of a highly literate and civilized nation. That was an emperor of a country which recognized tyrannical power. The difference was between pieces of deerskin and pieces of metal. But the morality was not different. Possibly the graven likeness of that remote emperor is still revered in China. And so is the "resolute" action of the American President still honored in stone, the written word, and in the oratory of his political party.

While Roosevelt's actions with respect to gold are more understandable because they are more sensational, the damage done was less harmful to property rights, to the security, and to the liberty of the American people than the various means which have always been available to the government through its control of money and credit. Since the great depression these means have been so consistently used by Congress and successive Administrations that they seem to be taken for granted.

In a valuable book for the average citizen, titled *What You Should Know About Inflation,* Henry Hazlitt offers the following concise definition of inflation: "Inflation, always and everywhere, is primarily caused by an increase in the supply of money and credit. In fact, inflation *is* the increase in the supply of money and credit." [4]

A rise in prices, often called inflation, is a consequence of inflation. First, there is a steady but not alarming rise in prices; then, because of a rising distrust in the stability of the government's currency, a disposition to exchange money for goods; finally, a headlong panic in which there is a flight from the currency into goods of any kind. That third phase is catastrophic. In Weimar Germany it facilitated a seizure of power by one of the most ruthless dictatorships in all history.

The procedure in the United States, as Hazlitt says, is basically a calculated increase in the amount of money and credit by the President and Congress. Under the laws of the United States,

[4] Princeton, N.J.: Copyright 1960, D. Van Nostrand Company, Inc.

which existed for two decades before the Roosevelt gold manipulations in 1933 and 1934, the government sells its bonds and other promises to pay to the banks. The banks book these IOU's as deposits against which the government can draw. A bank in turn can sell its government securities to the Federal Reserve Bank, which pays for them either by creating a deposit or by having Federal Reserve notes printed. This manufacturing of media of exchange differs little in effect from the crude process, practiced over the years by unscrupulous governments, of merely printing paper promises to pay and circulating such promises as money. The control of this process depends entirely upon the integrity of those in control of government. When that integrity is exercised in the interest of those who have money in savings, the expenses of the Federal government are kept within the revenues exacted by taxation. But when the government spends more than it takes in, the additional securities it prints and sells to the banks become a planned and calculated increase in the supply of money and credit.

Over the past thirty-one years we have had a balanced budget only six times. The net increase in the money supply is measured in the size of the national debt, now passing $300 billion.

In the first fifteen months of the Kennedy Administration, Presidential demands and Congressional compliance drove Federal expenditures to hitherto undreamed-of heights. As the fiscal year 1962 approaches its end, costs rise higher and higher. In March, 1961, the President forecast a $2.1 billion deficit for fiscal 1962. In May he revised this to $3.6 billion. Two months later the figure went to $5.3 billion. Then in January, 1962, when he submitted his annual budget, the estimate of red ink was $7 billion. The actual figure reported on June 30, 1962, was more than $7 billion.

Meanwhile, there was a request for Congress to raise the debt limit from $293 billion to $298 billion. The Secretary of the Treasury said that this was to be "temporary" and would raise "efficiency." But how temporary this will be can only be guessed. It proved to be "temporary" only on the top limit. For the need now is to raise the limit by $10 billion more. And the efficiency of the Administration can be judged by the fact that estimates of expenditures were consistently wrong.

This immense rise in spending cannot be charged entirely to military needs. For between 1955 and the estimated 1963 Presidential budget, requests for the military rose 30 per cent, while for all purposes the increase was 68 per cent.

Maurice Stans, who served as Budget Director in the final years of the Eisenhower Administration, wrote this warning in 1962:

We owe $30 billion in unfunded pensions to retired civilian employees of the government. We owe almost $40 billion in accrued pensions to retired military servicemen. The total of our present commitments to veterans for future pensions and compensation (not counting many other benefits) is in excess of $300 billion. All of this $370 billion is for past services and in the financial statement of a business would be accounted for among liabilities.

Then there are many other present contractual or legislated government undertakings that will have to be financed in the future. Taking all of them—housing subsidy contracts, shipping subsidies, the interstate highway system, unfinished public works projects, unpaid purchases of military supplies, and many others —this group adds up to more than $150 billion in further bills to be met in the coming years.

Altogether, counting the interest-bearing debt of $300 billion and the other obligations and commitments I have mentioned, we have placed a mortgage of over $800 billion on our national future to be met in taxes. This does not include untold billions of dollars in guarantees by the government on housing loans and other mortgages, bank deposits and other savings and so on.

Even this is not the full story. Under our Social Security system, we have scheduled a series of benefits that far exceed, in actuarial terms, the resources that would be available at present tax rates. This deficiency, which can only be made up out of future tax increases already provided in the law, is another $250 billion or $300 billion.

This makes the total present undertakings of the government, to be paid from future taxes, in excess of a trillion dollars.

All this must somehow be extracted from private production and savings through taxation.

There was considerable inflation prior to 1940, but for the sake of brevity we need only consider how great was the impact of inflation since that date. From the beginning of 1940 to the end of 1959, the cost of living increased 113 per cent; wholesale commodity prices, 136 per cent; and the total supply of bank deposits and currency, 270 per cent. No "shortage of goods" caused this increase. For industrial production increased 177 per cent.

We also hear a great deal of other causes of inflationary pressures, such as the "wage-price spiral." But, as Hazlitt says:

If it [the wage-price rise] were not preceded or accompanied by an increase in the supply of money, an increase in wages above the "equilibrium level" would not cause inflation; it would merely cause unemployment. And an increase in prices without an increase in the cash in people's pockets would merely cause a falling off in sales. Thus wage and price rises are usually the consequence of inflation.

One way to characterize inflation is in terms of the moral issues that it presents.

The most important moral wrong involved, and the one most commonly understood, is the fact that it is a process of literally destroying the value of savings which the individual has entrusted to government securities, insurance companies, and savings banks. This, of course, thwarts the individual's means of self-help and personal security.

Inflation transforms the normal transactions of business into speculative gambles, especially for small businesses which lack the means of hiring high-priced economic advice. Future commitments, plans, outlays, and contracts must be guided to a large degree by mere guessing as to how politics may affect values.

Inflation spawns demagogues who make the process of politics and government a compound of false promises, deceptions, hidden taxes, and unnecessary benefits.

Inflationary spending rots the fabric of constitutional government when Congress, as is its growing habit, bypasses public appropriations by authorizations to tap the Treasury. As Appropriations Chairman Cannon remarked, "While we are shoveling money out the front door, the spenders are carrying it out the back door of the Treasury . . . without let or hindrance."

When, inevitably, prices get out of hand, liberal economists promise controls, which in peacetime mean a reeking mess of black-marketeers, cheats, and hoarders, thus further polluting the moral atmosphere.

The nation's credit is the final, ultimate sacrifice. This means economic disaster, a consummation confidently predicted and eagerly awaited by Communism. If we thus fail, the world can have no peace.

CHAPTER 18

The Test of Competence

For a century after the inauguration of Washington there was little consideration and study of the competence of the Federal administrative establishment as against that of the smaller state and local units. The more perceptive and powerful minds of American statesmen were concerned with Constitutional questions involving relative powers. But in 1887, Woodrow Wilson, then a young college teacher, raised the question in an essay, *The Study of Administration.* He said:

I suppose that no practical science is ever studied where there is no need to know it. . . . It is a thing almost taken for granted among us, that the present movement called civil service reform must, after the accomplishment of its first purpose, expand into efforts to improve, not the personnel only, but also the organization and methods of our government offices: because it is plain that their organization and methods need improvement only less than their personnel. It is the object of administrative study to discover, first, what government can properly and successfully do, and, secondly, how it can do these proper things with the utmost possible efficiency and at the least possible cost either of money or of energy. On both these points there is obviously much need of light among us; and only careful study can supply that light.

Perhaps what had moved him to consider this subject was the rapid growth even then of the Federal bureaucracy. In 1861 there were only 36,672 civil employees, but when Wilson wrote his essay the number had multiplied four times.

In the years following Wilson's essay numerous individuals and agencies turned their attention to what some of them called the "science" of administration. The ideal of these pioneers was to create a standard of efficiency and training for government employees. But the rapid growth of government services at all levels frustrated these fine efforts. In large measure new bureaucrats learn their business on the job.

However, in part because of the influence of new means of measuring efficiency in private business, certain principles have been developed to measure administrative competence in government. One consideration is the relative competence of centralized versus decentralized units of government.

In one of the studies in a new volume called *Essays in Federalism* Professor Procter Thomson of Claremont Men's College offers some interesting observations on the relative efficiency of large and small units of governmental administration.[1] Thomson draws his conclusions in answer to these questions:

"Does the government do what it has to do at the lowest possible cost? Does it allocate its own resources wisely and does it minimize the cost that it creates for the private economy? Does government secure the ability and wisdom to make intelligent decisions about the great questions of public policy?"

For, as Thomson says, "Efficiency sits in judgment at all times and places and represents an implied rule of performance for head-hunters, pyramid builders and star-bound astronauts."

There are, as Thomson points out, undeniable advantages in large-scale administrative operations. But as size increases there

[1] This volume is a product of the Institute for Studies in Federalism at Claremont Men's College. This co-operative work was established in 1958 because of the efforts of the President of the College, George C. S. Benson. Dr. Benson has spent many years in the study of government administration both in his academic life and in official and semi-official bodies. In 1954 he was Research Director of President Eisenhower's Commission on Intergovernmental Relations.

is reached a point of optimum efficiency beyond which smaller units produce more public service for less money.

The following observations concerning the limitations of large Federal operations have been informed and strengthened by Thomson's excellent essay. But in the main they are stated as my own:

1. The larger the administrative unit, and the more numerous and varied its activities, the smaller the amounts of time which the chief can give to each. The policies and directives become more and more general and less effective. Since the chief must base his directives upon information, he must rely for that upon the very individuals he is supposed to direct. In our present Federal government the President and the major department heads become subject to the bureaucrats over whom they preside.

2. When there is a chain of command, the directing force at the top loses strength and authority as the chain lengthens. There is what is called in electrical engineering "line loss."

3. In a vast aggregation of bureaus there must be contacts among them on subjects which are related. Such contacts and liaisons increase in what Thomson calls a "factorial effect." Contacts increase geometrically with the number of bureaus.

4. C. Northcote Parkinson points out that the staff of a bureau will grow at a predetermined rate regardless of the work to be done. But the ingenuity of bureaucrats also operates to invent new work and thus enlarge their number.

5. The larger the number of bureaus and agencies, the greater will be the number of interbureau rivalries and jealousies. This is a potent source of energy and money wasted. In our Federal government, to cite only one of scores of examples, several bureaus and more than one department concern themselves with the welfare of children. Each struggles to acquire a larger share of the child's life and concerns.

6. Most Federal departments have tentacles in many states. Thus the "line loss" is accented by geographical distances.

7. All bureaus and departments have periodical spasms of conscience which call for new people to co-ordinate and study things. This means more bureaucrats and supervisors to check upon what other bureaucrats and supervisors are doing.

8. The difficulty of getting competent administrators from private life to serve in large affairs in government is an old story. Even when a first-class individual is induced to serve, the harassments by Congress, the mutual jealousies within and among the departments, and occasional abuse by the press terminate his public service.

9. Finally, the cost of bureaucracy is not all represented in the President's budget. For the bureaucracy inflicts upon private businesses a not-too-gentle rain of questionnaires, reports, and other papers which represent an added cost of operation to them and a considerable charge against the economic system.

10. Bureaus and departments, to survive, must proclaim their value to the public through an army of public relations people and press officers. More people in Washington hand out "news" than there are newspaper reporters.

Thomson concludes that "the advantages of large-scale operation are far less considerable for public than for private organizations, but the disadvantages apply with equal force to both." The check upon competence among private administrators is the inexorable rule of the market place. That measure is not present in government.

Another very important factor in measuring the competence of government is the dearth of means of discovering and evaluating high-grade administrative and technical talent. In the business world talent can be measured by the yardstick of the free market. Businesses fail or prosper in competition with each other. Individual managers are measured by demonstrated results. There are no such clear means of measurement in a bureaucracy. In fact, the web of regulations imposed under the Federal Civil Service is such that there is more protection for the incompetent than rewards for unusual talent. In a system which gives merits for conformity and demerits for a wrong decision, the pressure is to conform to routine, not to originate. For to originate is to take a risk.

Since the range of operations in the superstate is so great, there is inevitably not enough talent to go around. Hence there is terrific competition among the agencies of government for talent, and the success of one agency in corralling good men and women depends much more upon the machinations within the bureaucracy than upon any real determination of where such talent is needed most.

The fact is that whenever a new agency is created or a new and important service is to be performed, the President is more likely to entice a proved man in the business or scientific world than to depend upon what he already has. And when such a proved individual is convinced that he must take an official assignment on the grounds of good citizenship or public service, his stay is usually short. In a year or a few years the edge is worn off, the frustrations in the bureaucracy are so trying and the influence of politics so great that he returns to private life.

Presidents bitterly complain about their inability to secure competent people in private life to serve in public office. But the same Presidents ignore the fact that the reason why they cannot find people whose competence is adequate is that they have promoted the enlargement of their government to such an extent that it fails to attract enough talented people to operate it.

In 1921, in the Budget and Accounting Act, Congress established a General Accounting Office with the Comptroller of the United States as its head. He reports directly to Congress. This official was made independent of political changes by a fifteen-year term. But for many years the Comptroller and his office were devoted almost entirely to an auditing operation of all expenditures. This was mainly a routine task to determine whether such expenditures were made in accordance with the law. The parallel responsibility of the office, to consider the efficiency with which administrative operations were conducted, was lost in the routine of audit. However, when Joseph Campbell was appointed to the office in 1955 there was a change. No Comptroller in the forty years' history of the office has been so vigorous and searching in his surveillance of Executive operations.

Some of the Comptroller's audits are conducted on his own initiative as a part of his statutory responsibility. Others are at the request of the officers of Congress, Congressional committees and subcommittees, and individual members. There are also informal contacts with committees and members, and there are also occasional contacts with the Director of the Budget.

In 1961 there were 5,752 such reports and contacts. These ranged over the entire operations of the government at home and abroad. In these reports the Comptroller and the other employees of the General Accounting Office vigorously and courageously pointed out to Congress and the public hundreds of examples of deficiencies, waste, incompetence, and neglect.

In any one of the years since Campbell has been in office these blue-covered reports have collectively been a vivid chronicle and a forceful reminder of the loose ways which are characteristic of the bureaucracy's management of public affairs. They portray the waste of hundreds of millions of dollars and countless man-hours through blunders and miscalculations.

This lesson from the stacks of blue reports and the annual reports of the Comptroller is brought out with concrete and detailed evidence. Many of the examples of incompetence and waste lie in the realm of plain common sense. With the advent of all-encompassing government, individuals who operate the bureaucracy progressively lose their standards of balance, their intelligence, and even that decent respect which they owe to the nation which they serve.[2]

[2] For the proof of this general statement I refer the reader to the Annual Reports of the Comptroller General since 1956.

CHAPTER 19

The Moral Consequences

In the American character, individualism and the Judaeo-Christian ethic were brought together harmoniously. While the metal that went into it came across seas and oceans, it was pounded out on a new anvil—a continent stretching from the Atlantic Seaboard to the Alleghenies, across the Great Plains to the Rockies and on to the South and West, to the Rio Grande and the Pacific.

Those who came to these shores struggled with adversity and for uncertain fortune. They were, with some exceptions, courageous, dedicated individuals. Whether they came to escape the grinding oppressions of Europe, its galling authorities and its bane of class, or in search of opportunity, their actions bespeak these virtues. They gained individual liberties which men have always sought and still seek. Those who stayed here and survived came to find that the religious ethic had as great a validity on the American frontier as in the most desperately impoverished neighborhood in Europe. Their object was worth the quest.

But certain consequences of our basic ethical principles have become apparent as collective interests have increasingly curbed individual enterprise. The cult of the "environmentalists" has lessened emphasis on individual responsibility. This trend has been compounded by the recognition in politics of a vote-getting value in the shifting of responsibility to government, in care for the maintenance of every individual's special welfare, and in redistribution of income and wealth. The Federal government has rapidly seized upon responsibilities which were earlier those of individuals, of families, of private agencies, and of local and state governments. And today a national political party claims a monopoly in these matters.

In his *The Freudian Ethic*, Richard LaPiere describes this trend:

It is already evident that political maternalism has thrown the social balance against the man of enterprise, erected many discouragements to the generation and expression of individual initiative. . . . With each extension of political maternalism the individual is devaluated, and organization—in this case political —is exalted; for with each such extension some class of individuals is deprived of the pre-existing right to determine, for good or ill, their own conduct in some respect or other. As this right is taken from individuals and nonpolitical organizations of individuals, it is transferred to some centralized political authority . . . [which] makes for the forcible homogenization of the members of society. . . . Now we find a society—our own—beginning to abandon the universal principle of reciprocity and to provide through political means for the maintenance of a potentially unlimited number of members who are not required either to have contributed or to be likely in the future to contribute anything— material or otherwise—to the society. It is now quite possible for a reasonably determined irresponsible to progress, from childhood through youth and maturity and into old age, from welfare agency to welfare agency and from this social provision to that, without having made more than a token effort to take and hold a remunerative job.[1]

The impact of liberalism upon American character manifests itself in the impairment not only of government itself but of the political parties, of society, and of the individual.

Over the centuries many governments have considered themselves bound by none of the moral imperatives recognized and

[1] (New York: Duell, Sloan and Pearce, 1959), pp. 262, 265, 279.

practiced by honorable individuals. Men acting together in a community, a faction, or a class in that collective entity known as the state have in the name of king, ruling class, or majority not only condoned but promoted public activities alien to honorable behavior between individuals.

Dishonesty in economic affairs and the ruthlessness of the Congress and the bureaucracy in denying individuals the product of their labor and ingenuity and intelligence are as callous as the actions of an enraged mob, although violence is absent. The important difference is that in a mob reason is unseated. Governments commit their depredations in cold blood and by calculated means. And their rationalizations merely compound their evil by hypocrisy. Fine words precede and follow foul deeds.

Within the protective shield of an apathetic electorate, the member of Congress will vote for laws which inflict upon individuals a wrong which he would never dream of committing in his private relations with his neighbor. The bureaucrat, shielded by law, becomes a minor tyrant.

Niccolò Machiavelli wrote some bitter observations on "how princes should keep faith." Four centuries ago he explained that "princes who have set little store by their word, but have known how to overreach others by their cunning, have accomplished great things, and in the end had the better of those who trusted to honest dealing." His evaluations of the statecraft of his time have been widely influential. Time has softened the manner of princes, but the substance has endured.

The growth of liberalism has also been marked by a departure from the traditional American ideal of a classless society. For a considerable number of years, the claim that a party represents all groups has been given only lip service. In practice, votes are snared in covies. Labor and other minority groups are collective targets of political appeals. Political deals with the leaders of these groups have supplemented general appeals to their members.

The crass materialism of the superstate is obvious. Cash benefits are traded for votes. Gifts individually bestowed, with which the old-fashioned political chief bought his majorities, have been supplanted by a downpour of government checks. The benign boss in a Prince Albert and cravat has made way for the glib college product in a two-button sharkshin and slim-jim. In political discourse "the good life" is used only in company with the flag and the Lord in the peroration. The substance is an array of promises. Not the good life, only the "goods of life."

Most important is the effect of liberal practices and policies on the fiber of individual Americans. Those who retain their capacity to work after they reach the age when social security payments begin have a limit set on their earnings. The unemployed are no longer expected to move to job opportunities; they must be supported where they are. Only the unusually self-reliant and enterprising farmer finds new ways to gain his subsistence from the soil. Ingenuity, innovation, and enterprise are thwarted by subsidies. Cities and states, deprived of tax sources and lacking the initiative to plan and to build, go hat in hand to Washington. If a city desires new public facilities, it does not demand them from its landowners through adequate land taxes. It acquires Federal urban renewal gifts or loans. Because of greed for Federal road-building funds, states risk bankruptcy in meeting their fraction of the cost. Crutches lean in every corner.

With the powerful support of Federal policies and legislation, labor demands not only a legitimate share in the earnings of modern industry, but fewer and fewer hours of work and more government-planned leisure. In one of Walter Reuther's excursions into national policy he favors more Federal aid to education with the content directed to "constructive and creative leisure."

Progressive education has long responded to this ideal. Emphasis on competition and striving for unusual achievement are frowned upon. "Adjustment" and "conformity to the norm" are the goals. LaPiere comments sharply that

the modern progressive educator accepts a philosophy of education that, if fully realized and actually effective, would produce high-school graduates totally incapable of living in society and prepared only to spend the rest of their lives on the analyst's couch. They would be passive, uncompetitive, unambitious, irresponsible, egocentric, and—of course—wondrously adjusted to doing nothing at all.[2]

In hundreds of high-school curricula hard courses in physics and mathematics, history, and English are crowded aside. Valuable, irretrievable time which should be devoted to the hard disciplines is given to instruction in grooming, junior homemaking for boys, teen-age square dancing, and other "projects." In better schools such leisure-time instruction is offered outside school hours.

If the United States stood alone in the world, this unproductive leisure might be safe. In a world of hungry nations, a world in which we seek to buy peace by sharing our wealth, a world infiltrated and threatened by an implacable enemy, this is outrageous folly. A nation producing less and less per capita is destined to disaster. A lavish accumulation of war-making equipment cannot save us. For without a strong, competitively sound economy such national defense cannot be sustained. Moreover, a citizenry infected with an unproductive way of life cannot supply the indispensable individual vigor to man our defense.

In a nation where government imposes heavy taxation for purposes which are not generally respected and with clever devices for collecting such imposts, the public responds with clever tricks of its own. Or there is a growth of plain cheating by rich and poor alike.

When inflation comes and controls are imposed, the moral

[2] *Ibid.*, p. 117.

decline is accelerated. Those who enforce as well as those who are subject to the law suffer a moral corruption. Contempt for authority grows. There is cynicism toward evil deeds in public office. Personal responsibility is eaten away. Criminal conduct, from unions and corporations to public servants, farmers, and small proprietors, becomes more frequent. It is small wonder that in a political climate which exalts the material above all, the citizens lose sight of moral and spiritual values.

The obsession of liberal democracy with mass security at the expense of individual enterprise is self-defeating. Risk-taking or venture is not in conflict with security. These two human instincts are correlative.

When we are young, or in high spirits, or when great prizes tempt us, an impulse to venture prevails. Venture requires energy and positive action. It is indispensable to progress. Venture is a risk taken for a known reward which may involve security. Thus, venture and security are interdependent. Each is indispensable to life. They create strong citizens and powerful nations. Reversed, with a quest for security first, what reward is there for venture, for ingenuity, for innovation?

We crave security when we are tired or ill or dispirited. And when times are out of joint, as in the great depression, security becomes a national slogan. It was that way when the flow of trade was frozen, when unemployment haunted workers, and when farming was profitless toil. Government began guaranteeing bank accounts, regulating investments, providing capital for business, and extending aid for the needy. These were essentials at the time. They were tonics for convalescence. Some, but not all, were considered at the time as patterns for the long future.

Ultimately, accent on security went too far. It fostered the delusion that security should be given, not earned. It frustrated the imaginative, driving spirit of youth. And to take that from the young is like taking the morning from the day.

Long ago, a most perceptive and sympathetic observer, Alexis de Tocqueville, warned Americans of the perils inherent in our democracy:

The species of oppression by which democratic nations are menaced is unlike anything that ever before existed in the world; our contemporaries will find no prototype of it in their memories. I seek in vain for an expression that will accurately convey the whole of the idea I have formed of it; the old words *despotism* and *tyranny* are inappropriate: the thing itself is new, and since I cannot name, I must attempt to define it.

. . . The first thing that strikes the observation is an innumerable multitude of men, all equal and alike, incessantly endeavoring to procure the petty and paltry pleasures with which they glut their lives. . . .

Above this race of men stands an immense and tutelary power, which takes upon itself alone to secure their gratifications and to watch over their fate. That power is absolute, minute, regular, provident, and mild. . . . For their happiness such a government willingly labors, but it chooses to be the sole agent and the only arbiter of that happiness; it provides for their security, foresees and supplies their necessities, facilitates their pleasures, manages their principal concerns, directs their industry, regulates the descent of property, and subdivides their inheritances: what remains, but to spare them all the care of thinking and all the trouble of living? . . .

The will of man is not shattered, but softened, bent, and guided; men are seldom forced by it to act, but they are constantly restrained from acting. Such a power does not destroy, but it prevents existence; it does not tyrannize, but it compresses, enervates, extinguishes, and stupefies a people, till each nation is reduced to nothing better than a flock of timid and industrious animals, of which the government is the shepherd.

We need not thumb back to ancient history to learn how a nation's character is weakened. The British character is still trying to recover from its bout with welfarism and socialism. The relative rate of recovery since the war in Britain as contrasted with that in West Germany and Japan is largely due to the massive governmental experiment in the former and the survival in the two defeated countries of the individual's capacity to work and work hard.

There is an old French saying that the stairways of time are forever echoing with the sound of wooden shoes going up and patent leather boots coming down. It is obvious that most parents have the inclination to overindulge their children. When this is confined to the families of individuals who have been successful there is no great injury to the nation as a whole, since there are many ambitious young people who have not yet acquired an aversion to struggle. But when the government itself conspires to follow the example of the misguided parent through a political policy on a national scale, the children of the poor as well as of the rich are made the victims. Disintegration becomes the rule and not the exception.

These moral consequences are foremost among the counts against the liberal ethic which through politics has become national policy. We may dissipate our material substance by waste at home and profligacy abroad. We may lose that respect among the nations which Americans earned when our power was but a fraction of what it is now. These losses would be recoverable under a government with different ideals.

But if in the course of protracted experiments with liberalism our strong individual fiber and character are impaired, the loss is total, irrecoverable, absolute.

THE CONSERVATIVE PROTEST

CHAPTER 20

The Dissenters

IT would be exceedingly pleasant to believe that there is abroad in the land an immense and rapidly growing protest against the liberal ideology and policies which I have described in the preceding chapters of this book. Then I could either enjoy the feeling that I am a voice, however small, of a thundering majority, or, flapping my wings like Chanticleer, be the harbinger of dawn. Or, better still, I would find it possible to forgo the labor of writing a book entirely and turn to less exacting pastimes.

The writing of an account of liberal excesses might then be like describing the Salem witchcraft scare—unpleasant, historical, but irrelevant to men's present interests and affairs. For under our electoral process correction would come automatically.

A long habit of self-discipline, however, has imposed certain inhibitions. I am not especially interested in being popular. Rather, it has seemed to me that my responsibility is to be realistic and, so far as my limited capacity will permit, to be right.

I do not know whether a majority of Americans are conservative within my definition of the term.

I have a very limited belief in polls. In a poll of a representative group of Americans, a great majority rejected socialism. But when the specifications of socialism were presented one by one, all were accepted.

Election statistics are somewhat more satisfactory, but in each separate case many collateral influences must be taken into consideration.

In such a vast population one meets and hears or hears from only a tiny few. And even when a sincere effort is made to ascertain the views of individuals, one must make allowance for the understanding, the veracity, and the circumstances which condition the answers. Alfred M. Landon, Republican candidate for President in 1936, had a habit of sounding public opinion by talking with taxi-drivers and hotel maids and waiters. On that basis, and despite his own distressing experience when he ran for President, he was induced to believe that Wendell Willkie would be elected in 1940.

In the 1961 campaign for mayor in New York City, I made it my business as an exercise in idle sampling to determine what the taxi-drivers thought of Mayor Wagner. They were, with only an exception or two, against him. Wagner was overwhelmingly re-elected.

There is, however, a conservative protest of indeterminate size, and there is reason to believe that it is stronger than it was ten years ago. Here are a few pieces of evidence.

There were the thirty-four million who voted for Nixon in 1960. Except for the majority vote in the 1956 Eisenhower election, this was more than had been cast for any Republican in history. The Kennedy vote was predominant only in the non-urban South and in Northern states where the margin was polled in large industrial centers. In Illinois the Kennedy edge will always be shadowed by well-based charges of fraud. But even there, Nixon ran far ahead of the Republican candidate for governor. So far as a religious element in the national vote was concerned, the advantages were about evenly balanced. In the large urban communities in the South, where Democratic traditions are disappearing, Nixon did very well indeed. Moreover, Nixon had none of the lustrous prestige of Eisenhower, but his vote was nearly as large as the General's in 1956. And his campaign was handicapped by many circumstances which are now well known.

There can be no doubt that millions who voted for Nixon believed, quite properly, that they were voting for conservative principles. This was shown in the tens of thousands of letters which he received after the election, letters to which I have had some access. In my own small grist of mail which came to me as a journalist, the same evidences were apparent.

There was also the wave of sentiment against the spending proposals in Congress in 1959 and 1960. Members hearing from home were measurably restrained. In 1961, in his honeymoon months, the President was not successful in winning Congressional support for his more liberal proposals. Witness the decisive vote against his aid-to-education plan in the House. In 1962 his proposal for an urban affairs department, an ultra-liberal measure, met decisive defeat.

In a subsequent chapter there is an analysis of voting records of Congress showing an increasing trend toward conservatism. In the election of 1960 the Republican Party made a substantial gain in House seats. But more important as an evidence of voter opinion in that election is the fact that the new members are generally conservative. Thirty-nine of the new members of the House in the 1961 session of the Eighty-seventh Congress registered more conservative votes than those of their predecessors. This was, of course, most marked in cases where Republicans succeeded Democrats. But even in cases in which there was no party change, new members' votes were, most often, more conservative than those of the people they succeeded. Moreover, Texas elected a Republican senator in 1961, the first since the Civil War.

Most significant, so far as the future is concerned, is the growth of active conservatism among college men and women and among young people generally. This is treated in the next chapter.

An ideological trend is always marked by the appearance of individuals and groups who are impatient with moderate elements and who, in actions and words, turn to more immediate and vigorous objectives. What is called the "extreme right" has captured a great deal of attention in the past two or three years. It is, like the more moderate drift toward conservatism, a reaction against liberalism in domestic and foreign policies. It attacks with little discrimination the policies of both political parties and those who represent those parties in government.

Extremes beget extremes. To a very considerable extent the "extremists of the right" react against the concessions of the wartime Roosevelt Administration and the postwar Truman Administration to the Soviet and later to the Chinese Communists. To a large degree, therefore, these people are reacting against a "soft" policy toward Communism. But their secondary concern is in opposition to the liberal policies of the Democratic Party. Because they are unwilling to associate themselves with either party, their attacks upon the Eisenhower Administration and Republicans generally have been severe.

Since the pronouncements of these extremists are in my opinion a gross violation of the true conservative tradition, I have expressed my dissent from the "extreme right" in a number of magazine and newspaper articles in the past three years. Each of these has brought me scores of letters of more or less violent disagreement. These have served only to deepen my conviction that such radicals injure the true conservative cause by providing valuable ammunition for the liberals.

They have been forcefully reproved by responsible Republicans generally, but this has served only to intensify their energies.

It is clear, however, that the cause of moderate liberalism and the Democratic Party has its own equally extreme elements. In March, 1962, a book entitled *The Liberal Papers* was published. This is in essence a series of suggestions for a radically modified policy toward Communism. In the "papers" which are presented, written by fifteen writers and professors, proposals are made which run counter to the foreign policies of even the Kennedy Administration. In essence, these people would sound a retreat by the United States from all of the trouble spots in the cold war against Communism. They represent surrender and appeasement. Such writings from individuals who have no official responsibility must be expected in a free society. But in this case, James Roosevelt, member of the House of Representatives from California, states that this manifesto grew out of an initial group of fellow-congressmen during the Eighty-sixth Congress in 1959–1960. This sponsorship is what is important.

Thus, both political parties are afflicted with the burden of extremism. It is an embarrassing burden, but an inevitable one.

CHAPTER 21

The Ideological Lag

POLITICAL issues, programs, and actions too often are compelled by fictions. Legends haunt our opinions. The realities of time and change quickly make myths of last year's problems. Politicians perpetuate such legends because the public mind with which they must deal is slow in comprehension. All too frequently the heroes and villains they feel called upon to portray are frozen figures, like the bodies of Lenin in the tomb in Red Square and of Stalin, now buried in a less conspicuous setting. The image of Mark Hanna was the caricature in the Hearst papers, a man with his clothing embellished with dollar signs—the ruthless national boss. The image of Governor John Peter Altgeld created by his enemies lingered, a man with bushy whiskers and a knife in his teeth—the anarchist. But Hanna was a man who esteemed rather than bossed President McKinley and who furthered, as much as any individual of his time, the cause of peaceful industrial relations. Altgeld was a sentimental man who, as Governor of Illinois, liberated certain individuals who had been convicted of participation in a riot not entirely of their making. Many years passed until more accurate portraits appeared in histories which few took the trouble to read.

But far more serious than these persisting distortions of individual character are the effects of an ideological lag upon living statesmen. There is a German saying that "things are faster than ideas." Formulas and ideological systems once exciting and fresh are applied long after the conditions for which they were created have passed.

The side effects, complications, and unanticipated problems to which a political ideology gives rise seldom concern the practitioner. Once in power, with his assorted social and economic nostrums, the politician will carry them to an extreme. He is reluctant to call a halt. He will not retrench. He is under pressure from his political benefactors and beneficiaries. Once the demagogue thoroughly hoodwinks his followers, they remain hoodwinked.

I believe that our basic political convictions—prejudices, if you will—are created at a rather early age, an age when we absorb the issues and political atmosphere around us. This age varies with individuals, but generally it is in the late teens or early twenties. For those who enter a life of politics, the ten or twenty years that follow see us rationalizing and documenting, perhaps slightly altering those basic leanings.

In the early New Deal the major policy-makers around Roosevelt, as well as the President himself, had come to political consciousness in the "Progressive" years preceding the First World War. Roosevelt was a Democrat and an admirer of Woodrow Wilson's New Jersey reforms. Roosevelt was profoundly devoted to his cousin Theodore and, in a sense, regarded himself as his ideological heir. There were also Henry Wallace and Harold Ickes, veterans of the Progressive revolt in the Republican Party. There was Rexford Tugwell, student of the firebrand Scott Nearing in his graduate studies at the University of Pennsylvania.

Thus, with people who twenty or more years before had been exponents of Progressivism in full control in Washington, the old plans for reform were brought out and refurbished. The early New Deal, from 1933 to 1936, was basically neo-Progressivism. There were semantic changes and a few additional concerns, such as personal-relief measures. But the outlines had been drawn long years before.

In the period preceding World War II another generation had come to maturity. Its political ideas were greatly influenced by the Roosevelt policies and personality. It is largely from that generation, grown to manhood in the late 1930's, that the Kennedy Administration has recruited its policy-making personnel. Kennedy himself attained voting age in 1938. Moreover, a large proportion of the liberal Democratic forces in Congress is of that same generation. Just as the early New Deal was neo-Progressive, so the New Frontier is neo-later New Deal.

Almost all the domestic policies and assumptions of the present Administration are derived from the second term of FDR. The patron saint of John F. Kennedy is Franklin D. Roosevelt. The present Administration's policies are dominated by the theory that by increasing government spending the rate of economic growth can be accelerated. Vast extensions of public power are proposed. Huge, ungainly welfare programs are now far beyond the daring expectations of Roosevelt himself. Business is to be more tightly regulated. And in foreign affairs certain shortcomings of the Roosevelt policies are compounded. Despite the rising threat of Communism, the foreign policies of the Kennedy regime are cautious, conciliatory, and lacking in clear line and definition.

A very important manifestation of the ideological lag which is pertinent here exists in our colleges and universities, where most of the teachers of the social sciences are in the same age range as the most prominent members of the Kennedy Administration. They, too, share a stereotyped attitude. Some of the more ardent supporters of the Kennedy policies in Congress come from that academic fraternity whose dismal teaching of economics, political science, and sociology is slanted toward liberalism. And indeed a very considerable proportion of the professional writing fraternity has that same basic political philosophy.

On the other hand, many young people have attained political consciousness and maturity during and since the Truman years. To them the great depression is a tale told in the history books.

They have heard all about Roosevelt and his policies, but feel no kinship with him. Many never knew the Soviet Union as an ally and friend. They know international Communism as a hateful system and a threat to the United States and to peoples everywhere striving for freedom. A number of them have come to realize that the profligate spending of this and past Administrations is a burden for them to shoulder until they can pass it on to their youngsters.

There is now, as never before since the Progressive era, a definite conflict of opinion between these young people and their political elders. They are in considerable numbers calling themselves conservative and are searching for a constructive conservative faith. This spirit of revolt is not only inevitable but wholly desirable. In a championship of the basic principles of American constitutionalism they belong to the true revolution of modern times. They are the exponents of individual rights.

Vigorous conservative and Republican clubs have appeared in many colleges. They hold enthusiastic meetings at which the speakers are notable conservatives in Congress, from academic life, and from journalism. They publish periodicals expounding their views. A detailed account of these developments is given in *Revolt on the Campus* by Stanton Evans.[1]

National organizations of young people dedicated to conservative principles are most active today. The first of the Young Republican organizations developed before the Roosevelt Presidency. In 1935 these groups formed the Young Republican National Federation, still very much alive, dedicated to action through the Republican Party. In its annual conventions spirited debates and contests for office have taken place in recent years. Its declarations of principles have been increasingly conservative in tone. In 1957 the Federation took a decidedly conservative stand and began electing conservative officers.

Then there is the Intercollegiate Society of Individualists whose

[1] Chicago: Henry Regnery Co., 1961.

principles, while conservative in nature, are largely philosophical. The Young Americans for Freedom, formed in 1960, harbors specific political objectives. Its credo is definitely in the classic traditions of domestic conservatism, and also emphasizes a strongly anti-Communist foreign policy.

This acceptance of the great responsibility for the future is most encouraging. For these young Americans, especially those in college or recently graduated, have had the privilege of education. From these will come the will, energy, and intelligence to ignite and strengthen the conservative tradition in America in the next generation. In a very few years these young people will be a powerful, indeed decisive, factor in politics. They will supply leaders in public affairs and government. They will be writing the books, gathering and editing the news, teaching in the schools and colleges, and preaching in the pulpits to another generation.

CHAPTER 22

Mood and Method in the Conservative Tradition

CONSERVATIVES in the 1960's need not and should not exhaust their energies in mere protest. For it is their mission to be the proponents of an illustrious tradition and the active agents of durable future progress.

The conservative in that tradition has been distinguished by his shrewd evaluation of the capacities and limitations of his fellow man. This estimate has determined his methods and shaped his principles of statecraft.

We Americans quite properly find the roots of our traditions in the American Constitution and in the colonial and state governments which preceded it. But our leaders in that period were at one with their contemporaries in the Whig Party in the mother country. The greatest of their British contemporaries was Edmund Burke.[1]

The mood of such American statesmen as Madison, John Adams, Hamilton, and James Wilson can best be portrayed by reference to the incomparably articulate Burke. Burke was the greatest spokesman of his time for the truly great revolution in modern times, constitutionalism.

[1] I am not concerned here with the discussion, so well presented in Hayek's *Constitution of Liberty,* as to whether Burke should be called a Whig, a liberal, or a conservative, since that author's point of view on semantics is so largely influenced by Continental concepts and ideologies.

Every American schoolboy knows, or used to know, Burke's memorable defenses of the American colonies in the years just before the American Revolution. These stressed, above all else, the unity in thought and purpose between the English who came to America and those who remained behind:

The people of the colonies are descendants of Englishmen. England, Sir, is a nation which still, I hope, respects, and formerly adored, her freedom. The colonists emigrated from you when this part of your character was most predominant; and they took this bias and direction the moment they parted from your hands. They are therefore not only devoted to liberty, but to liberty according to English ideas and on English principles.

He therefore concluded, in his arraignment of the government he opposed, that an Englishman "is the last man in the world" to deny the rights of another Englishman.

Burke fought to the end to impress the benighted Tory government with the necessity for conciliation with the colonies. He sought to show that a settlement could be had by a recognition of the traditional rights of men of common blood and ancestry.

Much later, in the final years of his life, Burke restated his constitutional principles in his denunciation of the French Revolution. Only the most superficial historians have found inconsistency between Burke's defense of the American colonies in 1765 and 1775 and his arraignment of Jacobinism in 1790. In both instances there is apparent the mood which so distinguishes the conservative. Burke abhorred violence. He held sudden change to be inconsistent with progress under liberty. In both instances his wisdom was proved to be right. The British lost their most valuable ties with the future in the American Revolution, and the excesses of the Jacobins brought their nation to dictatorship and disaster.

Burke believed in reform, however, and many of his lesser-known speeches and letters were urgent appeals for the abandonment of outworn practices and policies. But reform, he believed, should be consonant with a realistic appraisal of human nature. "In what we reform we are never wholly new, in what we retain we are never wholly obsolete." Also: "Those who attempt to level, never equalize."

He was the enemy of arbitrary power in any form—in a king, a government, or a majority. But in curbing arbitrary power he held that "there is always a better remedy . . . than civil confusion."

Basically, his political faith was rooted in his religious interests. A constitutional order must work "after the pattern of Nature."

More than a century later, a perceptive and learned Englishman summed up the conservative mood as it had prevailed over the generations of British politics:

Conservatism sees men not under a political but under a cosmological order. Politics is therefore a means to an end beyond politics. It is not that the Conservative is more religious than other men, but that he is less confident than some other men about man's self-dependence, more inclined to mistrust the finality of man-made remedies for human ills, more prone to look for the source of these ills rather in a defective human nature than in defective laws and institutions. This peculiar scepticism about political or economic remedies for all the ills of human flesh, is at its best re-inforced by an attachment to the moral free-agency of the individual. You *can* make men moral by Act of Parliament, but to what purpose if the operation of the law is merely external to the individual? . . . This is the highest ground upon which Conservatives resist the intrusion of state-power into certain spheres of the citizen's life. Conservatism champions that diminishing thing, "the private life," not as a form of escapism but as a sphere of moral free-agency.[2]

After the passage of the Reform Bill in 1832, the tradition of Burke found a party home in the new Conservative Party. Sir Robert Peel founded the party in his determination to effectuate

[2] R. J. White, ed., *The Conservative Tradition* (New York: New York University Press, 1957), p. 4.

the new order in national policies. The mood was conservative; the method was rational and moderate.

Then Benjamin Disraeli succeeded Peel as head of the Conservative Party. Disraeli took his appeal from the dismal science of economics, as it had been expounded by Bentham and others, to the supreme tribunal of patriotism. In a fine appraisal of Disraeli's statesmanship, André Maurois says:

A nation is a work of art, a work wrought by time. It has a temperament like that of an individual. The greatness of England in particular is sprung, not from its natural resources, which are mediocre, but from its institutions. The rights of Englishmen are older by four full centuries than the Rights of Man. . . . The duty of a conservative leader was to have the courage to defend the past so far as it was living and likely to live.[3]

That Disraeli's statesmanship was in the very pattern of progress was shown by the fact that he, rather than the Liberal Gladstone, forced through Parliament the second great Reform Bill in 1867.

This concept, which has been called by some "Tory democracy," has prevailed for a century since. It has been the faith of Churchill and Macmillan in our time. In the vicissitudes of politics, the British Conservatives have been frequently shaken by internal conflict and foreign diversions. But essentially the mood and method have remained. Perhaps their greatest trial was in assuming control after six years of socialism in 1951. Here their problem was to make the best of things. The social services were embedded in national policy, and so they accepted most of them but measurably rationalized them to ease the burden on a slowly reviving economy. Nationalization was stopped in its tracks. The burdens of the cold war were assumed. And now, despite the wails of the extreme Tories, Britain is recognizing new forms of trade and commerce in a changing world.

[3] *Disraeli, A Picture of the Victorian Age* (New York: D. Appleton and Co.. 1928), p. 106.

In the United States many circumstances have prevented the rise of a political party authentically dedicated to the conservative tradition. For many reasons, conservatives were until the last three decades scattered between the two major parties. The failure of those conservatives to make common cause was due to the tremendous consequences of the issue of slavery and the status of the Negro. But in our time the realignment may well be possible, provided there is leadership within the Republican Party endowed with the courage, sagacity, and wisdom to grasp this opportunity.

THE REPUBLICAN ALTERNATIVE

CHAPTER 23

The Republican Party Today

THIS is the thesis of succeeding chapters of this book: If the opposition to Democratic liberalism is to establish itself in a position to create national policy, it must do so through political action. In the United States political action must be channeled through the two-party system. The alternative is offered by the Republican Party.

But many sincere people question whether the Republican Party is worthy of their support. This question involves several subsidiary questions:

1. Are there other alternatives?

2. Is the Republican Party as it is now represented in Congress or elsewhere capable of providing a suitable alternative? Is its representation in Congress effectively united in a real opposition to Democratic liberalism?

3. Is there a potential in the electorate which could assure the Republican Party victories at the polls to gain control of the Federal government?

One suggested alternative is to create a new "conservative" party with perhaps another name. This, on the basis of past experience and present conditions, is utterly impractical. No new party has emerged as a major party since the Republican Party was born more than a century ago. At that time, the Whig Party was in a state of collapse, with its great leaders dead and its organization reduced to impotence. Also, a tremendous antislavery issue of national importance had emerged. Since then, third parties have been shortlived.

A new national party would have to create organizations in fifty states. In those states and in the Federal government there is a mass of laws generally based upon the party system as it now stands. These laws provide built-in advantages for Republicans and Democrats. In a majority of states the Republican Party is fairly well organized and holds offices down to the township and precinct level.

A splinter conservative party in a state serves only to elect liberal Democrats. Indeed, in Utah in 1958, it was personal antipathy toward a Republican senator by an ultraconservative that resulted in the election of an extreme liberal Democrat. In New York in 1962 a group of unhappy conservatives are, at this writing, attempting to create a new state party for the express purpose of defeating the Republican governor and a United States senator. It seems to be of small concern that the outcome of this effort may be the election of still more liberal Democrats.

Those who believe that "things must get worse before they get better" are utterly deluded. With liberalism in the ascendancy there is no time for such folly.

Another type of misguided conservative indulges in what has been called "delusive heroics." He says: "My conscience and principles cannot permit me to support a Republican Party which makes so many compromises." But he has no monopoly of principles. The maintenance of the two-party system is itself a principle of transcendent importance in preserving individual liberty and sound and stable government. The history of some modern states clearly shows that a multi-party system degenerates into a one-party system and then into a one-man government.

There are an increasing number of conservatives who, in their dissatisfaction with the two parties and the principles which those parties profess, create organizations to promulgate for public distribution printed material of an ideological nature. They believe that change in national policies can be effectuated by an appeal to the bar of public opinion in that way. Their publications have a certain educational value. But they are no alternative for those who choose to work within a party.

In my comment on these organized efforts I wish to make clear that certain educational and information agencies have great value and are generally quite legitimate in their influence upon public opinion. Thus, I would exclude from my criticism publications dealing with the interests of labor and business groups, with the field of education, such nonpartisan agencies as the Tax Foundation, and all sorts of other specific concerns.

I am concerned here with certain publications which appear in the form of pamphlets, magazines, and books which concern themselves with the broad political and ideological area. I cannot question their sincerity. I question their value in achieving the end they seek, which is to change the course of national policy in government.

So far as they are conservative in nature, they are almost wholly ignored by the liberals. Since these publications are read only by those who are already converted, and since they have detached themselves from the political arena, they constitute no threat to the party in power. So far as those who are either officially or otherwise in the Republican Party are concerned, these independent critics are generally considered to be wasting their time. And in influencing mass opinion they are negligible, because they reach such a minute part of the vast voting population. Indeed, since they advocate no form of political action at all, they are regarded by those who do believe in conservative political action within a party as a wholly negative force. Also, so far as their puny influence is concerned they do more harm to the conservative cause than good. For they are all bark and no bite.

The individual in public office who is at the moment most admired by American conservatives is Senator Barry Goldwater. In the Republican convention in 1960 he was the choice for the Presidential nomination of a number of delegates and of many rank and file Republicans. But when it became apparent that the nomination of Nixon was assured, he made an eloquent plea for solidarity behind the choices of the convention. Unfortunately, there were many who failed to heed those words, perhaps enough to have turned the tide on election day. While these individuals were complaining about what Nixon said or failed to say, the Democrats closed ranks and mobilized the votes. Thus, those irreconcilable conservatives assured a national regime which represents an ideology against which they now so furiously rage.

Conservatives as well as liberals must come to realize that no candidate can satisfy everybody in his party. In weighing his choices, the voter must consider not only the candidates but the welfare of his party and the nation.

I am constantly reminded by those with whom I discuss politics of the wide differences within the party as it is represented in Congress. "How," they say, "can either party stand for principles when it has such divergent members as Javits and Goldwater or Thurmond and Humphrey?" But such deviations are not numerous in the two parties now in Congress. A big party can afford its eccentrics, just as can a church, a race, nationality, college faculty, or club. Differences between Javits and Tower, for example, are due to the special conditions in the states which they represent. But in general principles they can find unity.

There is, however, a fundamental difference in ideology between the parties, and this is reflected more and more in the representatives of the parties in Congress.

Half of the people now living were not born when Franklin D. Roosevelt won over Herbert Hoover in 1932. Only one-fifth of the people now of voting age were able to vote that year. Only a shrinking handful of the present members of the House were there when Hoover was President. In the Senate, the senior Republican member in term of service is Alexander Wiley, who was first elected in 1938. He is followed in seniority by Senator Aiken, elected in 1940, and three members elected in 1944.

In the past ten years an increasing number of young Republicans have entered the House of Representatives. They are especially distinguished by their conservatism and their capacity to express their views. The future leadership of the Republican Party lies with that group—perhaps thirty or forty in number. In the Eighty-seventh Congress there were fifty-five new members, of whom fifty-three served throughout the first session. Three-quarters of these were, in their voting records in 1961, more conservative than their predecessors.

In the South the long era of exclusively Democratic rule is ending. An entire generation has appeared which cannot remember or can only dimly know of the circumstances which justified the exclusion of the Republican Party from that region. Time is crumbling the bony hand of hate in Southern politics. The Negroes, over whom the secession from the Republican Party started, are now voting in the South as well as the North against the party of the Great Emancipator. It is liberal Democracy which is now exploiting the issue of civil rights. In the South five major cities voted for Nixon in 1960. Republicans are appearing in Congress from districts which ever since the Reconstruction were Democratic. Texas has elected its first Republican senator. Thus it is evident that conservatives in the South are drifting into the Republican Party.

In a very revealing analysis of key votes in the Eighty-sixth and Eighty-seventh Congresses by *The Congressional Quarterly*, it is clear that the Republican minority in Congress is moving more and more toward consistent opposition to the enlargement of the Federal government. In the Eighty-sixth Congress Democrats supported an enlargement of Federal power "almost four times as often as Republicans." In the first session of the Eighty-seventh Congress Democrats supported an enlargement of Federal power five times as often as Republicans.

The essential cohesion of the Republican Party on conservative issues is shown in a very comprehensive study by Stricker Research Associates, Inc., a highly reliable private research agency. This study covers the voting records of all members of Congress in the 1961 session of the Eighty-seventh Congress. It is much more comprehensive than studies hitherto made by the AFL-CIO's Committee on Political Education, the Americans for Democratic Action, and the Americans for Constitutional Action. While those other surveys considered only from 10 to 18 roll calls, the Stricker study is based upon 115 roll calls in the Senate and 40 in the House. It is more precise than the others in that it measures the attitudes of members mostly on amendments to bills rather than final passage. This was done because a member will often vote his convictions on amendments but on the final passage of a bill vote for it on the "half-a-loaf" principle.

The measures considered concerned the centralization and enlargement of the power of Federal government, government intervention in labor relations and the private economy, and fiscal responsibility and spending. The study does not consider foreign affairs except where they would have an impact upon the foregoing domestic issues. Civil rights votes are not considered, nor are procedural matters.

The study ranges the members in a wide spectrum, from conservatism to liberalism in the sense in which these words are used in this book.

To show the range of party differences in the Stricker study, I have divided the members of each house into three groups. In the Senate there are, in the more conservative group, twenty-four Republicans and eight Democrats. In a middle group are nine Republicans and seven Democrats. In the more Liberal group are two Republicans—Javits of New York and Case of New Jersey—and forty-eight Democrats.

In the House there are 176 members in the more conservative group—155 of whom are Republicans, and 21 Democrats. In the middle group there are 31 members, of whom 13 are Republicans and 18 are Democrats. In the more liberal group there are 4 Republicans and 217 Democrats.

Thus, on issues of substantial ideological significance there is a concentration of Republicans in the conservative and of Democrats in the liberal sectors. It is very marked in this Congress, far more than in any period in modern times.

The lesson in this should be clear to conservatives who choose to shun party allegiance. There is a lesson also for those who call themselves "independent" because of their claim that "there is no difference" or because they have no political principles or are just plain timid. There is a party which they can join and work and vote for. There is no valid argument for such abstentions. Those who do abstain are gravely injuring the vitality and health of a two-party system.

Because of the traditional conditions in the South, there are more deviators in the Democratic Party than among the Republicans. This is shown in the study, although issues involving racial relations are not included.

These figures should show all reasonable conservatives that they can and should find a party home in the Republican Party. Those who are still irreconcilable must remain not only hopeless but impotent.

CHAPTER 24

The Republican Potential

THE clamor of minorities is so vehement, their organized efforts so well directed, and their special interests so skillfully advocated that many political leaders discount or ignore the great majority who must bear the burdens of the superstate. The claims of that majority are not dramatic. Its leadership has been lacking. It has no organization, And so it is forgotten.

Years ago, William Graham Sumner asked in an essay, "Who is the Forgotten Man?"

. . . The Forgotten Man is delving away in patient industry, supporting his family, paying his taxes, casting his vote, supporting the church and the school, reading his newspaper, and cheering for the politician of his admiration, but he is the only one for whom there is no provision in the great scramble and the big divide. . . . He works, he votes, generally he prays—but he always pays—yes, above all he pays. . . . He keeps production going on. . . . He is strongly patriotic. . . . He is not in any way a hero . . . or a problem . . . nor notorious . . . nor an object of sentiment . . . nor a burden . . . nor the object of a job . . . nor one over whom sentimental economists and statesmen can parade their fine sentiments. . . . Therefore he is forgotten.

The purpose of this chapter is to define in terms of the 1960's those who conform to the type described by Sumner. They are the potential fulcrum of political power. They are the Republican potential.

In an earlier book, *How to Keep Our Liberty*,[1] I described with considerable elaboration what I called "the middle interests" in the United States. I do not, and should not, speak of classes in our society. Its diversity, its extreme fluidity in which movement of individuals from one income group to another is constant, the relative absence of real barriers to ambition and competence, and our fundamental equalitarian traditions have prevented the hardening of our society into the strata which prevail so generally over the world. The impervious walls of caste in India, the stubborn distinctions in England, and the new class forms under Communism are alien to our nature.

Let us consider certain broad aspects of the middle interests—first, in terms of income and occupation, then in terms of property, and, finally, in terms of certain nonmaterial values which they cherish and in which they should find unity.

The data which follow reveal the fallacy of the Marxian thesis, shared by many liberals, that the rich are getting richer at the expense of all others. They show, on the contrary, that the so-called middle class, marked for extinction by Marx, is not a "class" at all in the sense of a minority of the population sandwiched between an upper crust of aristocracy and a thick slab of proletarians.

Whereas a little over a decade ago the bulk of our voting population and the center of political power were families with incomes ranging between $2,000 and $5,000, these statistics indicate that the middle income group in 1960 was centered between $4,000 and $10,000, constituting 54 per cent of the nation's families. Those families with annual incomes below $4,000 were 32 per cent, and those above $10,000 were 14 per cent of the total.

The following table from the Department of Commerce's *1961 Current Population Report on Consumer Income* gives a breakdown of the number of families by family income in 1960:

[1] New York: Alfred A. Knopf, 1952. Certain portions of this chapter are taken from that book.

Family Income	Number of Families
Total	45,435,000
Under 1,000	2,285,000
$1,000 to $1,999	3,613,000
$2,000 to $2,999	3,970,000
$3,000 to $3,999	4,456,000
$4,000 to $4,999	4,773,000
$5,000 to $5,999	5,839,000
$6,000 to $6,999	4,889,000
$7,000 to $7,999	3,973,000
$8,000 to $9,999	5,135,000
$10,000 to $14,999	4,795,000
$15,000 and over	1,707,000

Increased average income and an impressive upward shift of families along the income scale have been consistent since the Second World War. The median income of families rose from $3,000 in 1947 to $5,600 in 1960, measured in current dollars. Despite the rise in consumer prices, in terms of constant 1960 dollars the rise was from $4,000 to $5,600, an increase of 40 per cent.

How have various groups fared in pursuits that would place them in "classes" abroad? In 1960, families whose head was a craftsman or foreman received a median total money income of $6,514; those whose head is a clerical or kindred worker, $5,953; professional or technical worker, $8,390; craftsman in construction, $6,272; laborers, except farm and mine, $4,315; sales workers, $6,954; teachers in elementary and secondary schools, $6,964; and service workers, excepting those in private households, $4,728.

Turning to average income for families whose head is in a major industry group, we find that families associated with mining have a nation-wide average of $6,189; with transportation, $6,712; retail trade, $5,486; finance, insurance, and real estate, $7,043; and wholesale trade, $6,325.

The conclusion to be drawn from this is that there has been a significant process of readjustment from the lower incomes of prewar years. This has pushed wage earners into the middle groups, a process that should create fundamental changes in their political sympathies and outlook.

Today, five out of ten American families have assets worth $5,000 or more, and one out of ten has assets worth $25,000 or more.

In 1950 individual savings amounted to $216 billion; by 1958 the figure had reached more than $345 billion. In 1952 there were 6,490,000 individual shareowners in American corporations. By 1962 there were 17,010,000. In 1962 proprietors, managers, and officials held 16.5 per cent of the stock; professional and semiprofessional people 14.0 per cent of the stock; clerical and sales workers, 18.2 per cent; service workers, 2.6 per cent; craftsmen and foremen, 5.7 per cent; farmers and farm laborers, 0.4 per cent; and operatives and laborers, 2.7 per cent. Housewives and nonemployed adult females accounted for 33.6 per cent, and nonemployed adult males held 6.3 per cent.[2]

In 1949 the total amount of life insurance in force was $213,-672,000,000. In 1960 it was $586,448,000,000. In 1950 there were 88 million policyholders, having 202 million policies, and the coverage per family was $4,600. In 1960 there were 118 million policyholders, having 282 million policies in force. The coverage per family had risen to $10,200.

In 1960 almost 60 per cent of America's nonfarm families lived in homes of their own, as against 50 per cent in 1950.

Considering where the bulk of the national income is located, it is obvious that the burden of taxation falls most heavily upon the middle incomes specified. This is made clear in the following

---

[2] I hope every Republican interested in organization in his party will take note of the foregoing figure of the percentage of corporate stocks owned by "housewives and unemployed adult females." It is the largest of all the groups owning the industry of the nation. Thus, there is forcefully pointed out the importance of mobilizing the potential of women in political work. They are at once the people who have the most time to do party work and also have the most to conserve.

table, which shows the amount of income tax, after credits, paid by the various income groups.

INCOME TAX AFTER CREDITS, IN MILLIONS OF DOLLARS *

ADJUSTED GROSS INCOME CLASS	1950	1958
Under $600	—	—
$600 to $999	40	38
$1,000 to $1,499	197	190
$1,500 to $1,999	413	306
$2,000 to $2,499	648	467
$2,500 to $2,999	891	672
$3,000 to $3,999	2,177	1,998
$4,000 to $4,999	2,044	2,945
$5,000 to $9,999	3,984	13,389
$10,000 to $14,999	1,157	4,291
$15,000 to $19,999	758	1,757
$20,000 to $49,999	2,503	4,270
$50,000 to $99,999	1,517	2,107
$100,000 to $199,999	942	981
$200,000 to $499,000	603	516
$500,000 to $999,999	240	175
$1,000,000 and over	261	233

* Treasury Department, Internal Revenue Service; *Statistics of Income.*

From these figures it is evident that in eight years the burden of taxation shifted significantly as more and more people moved into the middle interests group mentioned earlier. Taxes from those with an income of from $4,000 to $10,000 rose steeply from 33 per cent to more than 47 per cent of the total. Those paying taxes with incomes below $4,000 paid only between 10 and 11 per cent, whereas eight years before they carried 23 per cent of the total. The percentage of the burden carried by those with incomes above $10,000 remained about the same, shading off slightly from 42 per cent.

A consideration of "who's who" in the middle interests in any typical American community of some size would include a growing proportion of the population of those engaged in all sorts of occupations, professions, trades, and business. Hence, there are material interests that should bind together those who share them in the generation of great political power. The reasons why this vast population exercises so little political power are manifold. In nearly every community people divide party-wise only in local elections or are inclined to adopt the innocuous label "independent."

But the great issues that concern us here have little to do with issues of local government. In such communities, divisions on local concerns destroy the capacity of the people to protect their real interests in the nation. Other reasons for their political weakness, of course, are indifference and ignorance. Frequently indifference results from a sense of frustration or of helplessness.

This concentration of attention on material matters does not imply that voters are moved only by such things. The economic interpretation of the motives that have made history has been greatly emphasized in the historical and political literature of the past fifty years. And it is certainly given great stress in practical politics.

But people are moved by many impulses. Men are endowed and share sentiments of idealism, loyalty, and pride associated with the home, the family, the local community, friends, ancestry, tradition, religion, and patriotism. These sentiments fill a large part of life. They give strength and a feeling of well-being. They make hardships endurable, mistakes tolerable, and even failure bearable. To move the large, decisive segment of the middle interests to political action is a necessary job of inspired party and auxiliary work.

Liberalism under the new Democratic Party proposes a sterile, vitamined adequacy. The future is a flat plateau of uniformity over which ride the inspectors, regulators, and other officials of an uninspiring bureaucracy—an arid desert filled with mirages and the dry plants of demagogic jargon. A fare of subsidies, grants, wage escalators, a large assortment of government handouts, and welfare measures of all sorts is offered to satisfy the inheritors of a venturesome past.

The Republican can, if he will, base his appeal on a hundred inspiring values, on loyalties, on pride, on the treasured past, on what is lasting of the present, and on a bountiful and challenging future.

There are institutional ties, too—ties of infinite value to the middle interests and to all people. Most important is the American Constitution, the guarantor of a republican form of government, of limited government, of private rights, of the inviolability of the states, and of the authority of the judiciary. Together they make up a great body of tradition. They are surrounded by the atmosphere of freedom, of informed but recognized personal relationships, of local self-government, of social and economic custom, of a broad but not unlimited sense of equality, and of a spirit of live and let live, unshackled by law.

There has always been in our national character, moreover, an undying distrust of government, of unlimited tenure of office, of prying police and official presumption. Whether this trait has deteriorated is open to question. If so, it is a very dangerous change.

The Republican potential resides with those who share the fundamental interests described above, with those who hold these enumerated values dear, with those who can be brought to act politically.

CHAPTER 25

A Lesson from Britain

In 1950 I went to England to study the general election. I found there added substantiation for my conviction that the essential need of a successful party is efficient organization.

A few years before, in midsummer 1945, the Conservative Party had suffered a devastating defeat. It elected only 213 members of the House of Commons. Labor elected 399; other parties, 28. This astonishing result occurred despite the seeming advantage to the Conservatives of a victory in a war during which they had controlled the government, and also despite the immense popularity of the Conservative leader, Winston Churchill.

One British writer has said since that Conservatives "looked incredulously for an explanation for the 1945 defeat and decided that since their principles were immutable and unassailable, they must have been defeated by their machinery." This was quite true. For the party organization was in almost hopeless disrepair. Churchill had never given much attention to organization. He had believed that elections were won by the popularity of party leaders. But in 1946, after a year of reflection, Churchill turned to organization and to a man who, as he later said, had joined the Conservative Party as late as the day after the 1945 defeat. That man was Lord Woolton—Frederick Marquis before his elevation to the peerage. As an outstanding administrator he had spent nineteen years as the chief executive of Lewis's, a chain store organization in the north of England. With the coming of war he had joined the government as Minister of Food. Later he was Minister of Reconstruction.

In his early years, before he entered business, social work in Liverpool had absorbed his energies. He gave understanding helpfulness to the problems of workers, especially those employed at the docks. He believed that the improvement of their lot could best be achieved by enlightened business management, a sympathetic but not paternalistic government, and the opportunities for self-help rather than socialism. He was thus a true advocate of "Tory democracy."

Lord Woolton says in his *Memoirs* [1] that in 1946 his temptation was to tell the party that it should scrap the machinery and "start again." But as Chairman of the Conservative Party Organization he wisely decided that a new life could be created within the establishment as it stood. There was "no room for a Party dictator."

A headquarters staff, the "Central Office," under Woolton did not control the constituency associations, organized independently as the National Union of Conservative and Unionist Associations. Rather it served these associations. The Central Office's research department served the party ministers and Members of Parliament in matters of Conservative policy.

The constituency associations elected members to an Executive Committee with the chief Parliament whips represented. This committee met regularly to receive resolutions from the constituencies, and it conducted the annual party conference, "which was the much publicized 'mouth-piece of the rank and file of the Party.' "

In seeking his purposes within a disassociated structure, Woolton enlarged the pension fund which the party maintains for retired party professional workers and tactfully persuaded a large

---

[1] *The Memoirs of the Rt. Hon. the Earl of Woolton C.H., P.C., D.L., Ll.D.* (London: Cassell & Company Ltd., 1959).

number of them to seek a "well-earned rest." Then he brought into the party's professional service many talented younger men and women, often appealing to their patriotism to accept salaries smaller than they were earning in business and professional life. With an effective Central Office in London, Woolton was able to persuade the independent constituency associations to seek and select promising candidates for the House of Commons. Even more important, he encouraged the associations to employ a greater number of competent agents. The basis of Conservative success is the quality of more than six hundred constituency agents laboring throughout the United Kingdom. Training classes were created for equipping new agents for their heavy year-round responsibilities.

In 1948 the Swinton Conservative College was established in Yorkshire, providing, in the course of a year, political education to eighteen hundred students. This college was an important part of the educational activities of Woolton's Central Office.

The status of agents has been elevated by better salaries and by retirement provisions. It is the party's civil service. Woolton's objective of manning the constituencies with agents familiar with techniques of management and possessing qualities of leadership was advanced by recruiting retired army, navy, and air force officers. I have seen the training of these men put to excellent purposes of mobilizing Conservative membership, enthusiasm, and strength at the polls. A good agent also establishes committees in local communities of his constituency and trains a force of volunteers to assist during campaigns and at elections. He also organizes meetings and other contacts essential to money-raising at the local level.

Since the Central Office cannot adequately serve the needs of agents for advice and help, the United Kingdom is divided into a dozen regional areas with an "area agent" in charge of each, assisted by a deputy agent, generally a woman of experience.

Thus, the Central Office is able to maintain closer liaison with the many constituencies, their chairmen, and their agents.

From the first, Woolton sought to encourage the development of party alignment in local elections. Here he faced the problem so common in the United States—nonpartisanship. He was convinced that local councils are the training school for membership in Parliament and that vigorous local party organization is essential to success in a general election and for indoctrinating the electorate with Conservative ideas. In this he was eminently successful. In a visit to Birmingham during an election for the city council, I found the same party vigor manifested as in a general election.

Soon after his acceptance of the party chairmanship, Woolton decided on a bold step to get funds. He rejected the advice of other party leaders that a modest sum was all that could be squeezed from tax-burdened party stalwarts. But Woolton aimed at the high figure of a million pounds, and he got it from small as well as large contributions. This, he has said, gave the depressed party a "sense of accomplishment" and provided money to raise the standards of party workers and to carry on the publicity campaigns which played so large a part in the mobilization of Conservative strength in succeeding elections.

In 1948 at Woolton's suggestion the Conservative Party appointed a committee headed by Sir David Maxwell Fyfe to study and make recommendations for the organization. A major recommendation of this committee was that thereafter there should be no financial barriers to the support of candidates for the House of Commons. But the amount the candidate himself could contribute was limited. A new candidate could subscribe to his constituency funds twenty-five pounds annually; an incumbent candidate, fifty pounds. This radical change, Woolton believes, "did more than any factor to save the Conservative Party." These financial measures placed great responsibility upon the rank and file members. "People respect things for which they pay," Woolton observes. And they work and vote for a party in which they have an investment.

Throughout his *Memoirs* Woolton stresses what he called "Operation Knocker," a technique of personal contacts at the homes of the voters.

While socialism had grown to be a cult and a predominating influence in the British universities among dons and students alike, Woolton realized that Conservatism could be the mark of intellectual stature, and within two years the Conservative Party became dominant in the universities. It became a mark of distinction in the academic community, into which socialism had made such broad inroads, to be not only a dissenter from that philosophy but an articulate exponent of the Conservative Party.

In the five weeks which I spent traveling over the United Kingdom during the 1950 general election it became clear to me that, while most foreign correspondents were anticipating another big Labor victory, the strength of the Woolton organization was almost unnoticed. Labor elected 315 members, the Conservatives 298.

In the general election of 1951 the Conservatives took over the Government with a majority of more than twenty. In 1955 I again spent the weeks of the campaign in England and saw a Conservative victory, with a majority of sixty-five.

Following that election, the Labor Party acknowledged its inferiority in organization, and a distinguished committee reported:

After what we have seen of Party organization throughout the country our surprise is not that the General Election was lost, but that we won as many seats as we did. We were particularly disturbed by what appears to be the progressive deterioration of the Party's organization, especially at the constituency level. . . . As one M.P. put it to us, "When the tide is with us our bad organization relatively to the Tories doesn't matter; when the tide is against us our bad organization is fatal."

But apparently, despite the lecturing of Hugh Gaitskell and the recommendations of the committee, Labor Party organization failed to improve. I spent three weeks of the 1959 campaign in the Birmingham area. In that location alone seven Labor M.P.'s were defeated, and over the United Kingdom the Conservative majority exceeded 100.

Observe that in the elections of 1945, 1950, and 1951 the Conservative Party leader was Churchill. In 1955 it was Eden, and in 1959, Macmillan. Superior organization rather than the popularity of the Parliamentary leader made the great difference.

A great many Americans accept the somewhat superficial explanation that the British people rejected the Labor Party because its socialism had failed in the test of practice. These people also point out that the Conservatives accepted the welfarism so lavishly enacted by the Labor government after 1945. But while these have been factors, they fail to explain the reversal in Conservative fortunes. For while Labor had failed to accomplish all that it had promised, it still had a strong hold on the masses of British workers. While Conservatives since coming to power have continued social services, their administration of them has been both rationalized and limited. Much more important has been the capacity of the Conservative organization to carry to the British electorate the advantages of private enterprise, the greater degree of individual freedom which it assures in comparison with a planned economy, and the higher standard of living which has been realized under Conservative policies. This broad understanding could not have been attained without organized effort. And that organized effort was largely created by Lord Woolton, those associated with him, and his successors as party chairmen.

CHAPTER 26

Invigorating the Republican Party

THERE is an obsession—strange because it is expounded,
ad nauseam, by so many commentators experienced in politics
and by so many notable Republicans in or recently in high public
office—that all the party needs to return to power in Washington
are a number of attractive candidates and a batch of principles.
That such frail weapons can prevail over the use of Federal power
and financial resources by the most hard-riding and sagacious
Presidential machine since that of Jackson and Van Buren is
absurd. There is also the powerful auxiliary help of the political
arms of organized labor and racial groups to be considered. Two
successive elections of a Republican President failed to hold Congress and stem the liberal tide.

What is needed for Republican victories is an imaginative and
vigorous use of Republican assets at all levels. Following a great
deal of combing the minds of experienced politicians and calling
on my own observations and reflections over a number of years,
I shall in this and in the three chapters which follow make a
number of suggestions for invigorating the Republican Party in
Washington and over the nation.

A majority of these improvements can be made by the individuals who are officially in charge of the party now. Only one
or two would require changes in the laws governing party activity.
The latter might well be assured of adoption because they would
provide advantages for both major parties.

Theoretically, the Republican Party is represented at the top by the National Committee, which is composed of two members from each state, or three when a state chairman qualifies. The basic structure of the party is in the state, county, and other local committees and their chairmen and chairwomen.

Party Units in Washington

In Washington the National Committee maintains its national headquarters, with a full-time, mostly salaried staff. The National Chairman has his office there. The Republican Congressional Committee also has a full-time paid staff. The Senatorial Campaign Committee has a small, year-round operation. There is also the joint Senate-House leadership with a small but competent staff. Further, there is the Joint Committee on Republican Principles, which periodically drafts statements reflecting a Republican consensus on the party's present program for dealing with major policy problems which confront the nation. It endeavors to stress dominant themes for use in Republican campaigns.

A certain amount of co-operation among these party units prevails, but not as much as is needed if strong party leadership is to be maintained over the nation.

In describing what the staff of the National Committee should do, I am not assuming that there are not staff members who are engaged in most, if not all, of the activities I suggest. I am simply stressing certain indispensable functions of party activity.

A national political party should have at its head a full-time executive head, preferably salaried at a rate commensurate with his responsibilities. Such an individual should be primarily a highly competent executive. The evangelical function can be performed by the many official personages in the party, thus permitting the National Chairman to stay close to the staff in Washington.

But tradition has decreed otherwise. Chairmen have generally been unpaid and insecure in tenure. They have almost never been selected for their executive ability. Also, by tradition, the job has been regarded as a part-time vocation. There is, too, utter folly in the practice, also embedded in custom, of having a new chairman selected by the Presidential nominee after the national convention. Any business operation on such a pattern would be most unlikely to succeed.

In recent years the tendency has been to select a member of Congress as National Chairman, with the result that these already overburdened public servants must take on additional heavy duties. But since tradition seems too strong to break at this time, the National Committee should select a full-time, paid executive to serve under the chairman and keep store at headquarters in Washington.

Under that executive there should be departments to perform a number of activities. One should be charged with maintaining continuous contacts with state and local units of the party, assisting state and local chairmen with their operations, to the end that greater efficiency will be promoted by advice and suggestion.

Another should be charged with what might be called publicity and public relations. Within this division staff members should maintain contact with the press and other media. Part of this division might be called "operation gadfly," concerned with the release of material critical of the party in power or, if Republicans are in power, charged with presenting the achievements of the party. Thus, "pointing with pride" or "viewing with alarm" would be vigorously sustained.

Another division should be organized to create, publish, and distribute two publications at regular intervals, perhaps monthly. One would be a magazine, with competently written articles on public issues. This should not be a mere "throwaway" publication. Nor should it be a mere house organ full of pictures and "puff pieces" about party notables. It might be possible to make this journal pay a large part of its cost.

Another periodical, preferably a monthly, should be of the

"how-to-do-it" variety. Information about methods of organization could be channeled through this publication for the benefit of party and auxiliary workers over the nation. For example, if the chairman of the party in a certain city should develop an ingenious method of promoting registration or some other aspect of party activity, it should be described in this publication. This should be a professional journal available to party workers everywhere. It, too, might be partially supported by paid subscriptions.

The present speakers' bureau and women's division should be retained and strengthened.

Annual Conferences

Here I would most strongly urge emulation of the British system of annual party conferences. The office of the National Chairman should arrange and promote these affairs. Those attending should represent Republican members of Congress, governors, other major Republican public officials, all national committeemen and committeewomen, selected state chairmen and their co-chairmen, as well as all chairmen in the largest local communities. Also notable private citizens who are interested in the party should be invited. These conferences should be held during the Congressional recess, preferably in some spot away from the distractions of a large city. The sessions should last the greater part of a week.

These conferences should be organized with great care. It would be useless to program the affair exclusively with a few inspirational orators. The members should work together in round tables or committees to the end that there might be created an annual party manifesto stating points of agreement on current issues. Perhaps a resolutions committee could be appointed at the outset of the conference and after two or three days' deliberation it could present the draft of an acceptable manifesto.

It should be expected that there would be differences of opinion in such conferences. Divergent points of view should be well aired and submitted to orderly debate. The party could not be greatly harmed by such debates. Certainly, the British parties have not found themselves embarrassed by the publicized debates in their conferences.

So long as all members present are concerned with the success of the party, there is the probability of narrowing the differences by open discussion, despite the publicity which would ensue. To be sure, the manifestoes would represent some compromises, but they would have vastly more substance than the quadrennial party platforms which are hastily composed, seldom read, and soon forgotten.

Surely discussion of issues in such conferences, even if there are discords, would be preferable to a pernicious Republican habit, so common among orators at Lincoln Day dinners, of voicing criticism of their own party.

Party Finances

Whoever reads the suggestions for improving the organization of the Republican Party will ask the inevitable question, "Where is the money to come from?" For a bold and imaginative program costs money, and lots of it.

No one but the perennially fleeced "fat cats" will give to a party which suffers frequent defeats. It is most amazing, in fact, that the Republican Party is still able to finance its present operations. But the party must have more, and the base of its financial support should be widened.

Present and past methods of raising money in both Democratic and Republican parties have been wretched contrivances. There are the faithful, reliable contributors of considerable sums. Those givers, however, feel the pinch of many other demands upon their income, especially the exactions by the Treasury in tax payments. There are also contributions exacted from those who stand to gain from government contacts. This is a dubious contribution to efficiency and economy in public business.

Then there are the $100- or $50- or $25- or even $10-a-plate dinners. Those who purchase tickets for those affairs are either government employees, or loyal party supporters, or corporations with a special interest in the good will of the party in power. Those who buy the tickets, either in sizable lots or singly, are not always those who sit at the more or less festive board to listen to boring speeches by party luminaries. The tickets are largely given away by the purchasers.

A regular feature of such dinners is the presentation to the guests of a program filled with the advertising of companies or individuals who stand to gain from the party which demands a contribution. As legitimate advertising to sell products, the insertions are useless.

A party is an institution governed by law, but it is not a part of the government. It must live upon voluntary contributions of some sort. Large contributions provide the major support. Small ones are harder to get in large numbers but are better for the health of the party. This is because those who contribute only a small amount feel that they have an interest in the party and are more likely to work for its success at the polls.

Fully recognizing the wholly undesirable methods which were used to finance the two parties, Theodore Roosevelt proposed that they be financed by grants from the Federal government. Since then, many proposals of that character have been made. The argument for government financing is potent and, I believe, convincing. The two parties are essential to the process of government. Without their services the republic would dissipate into chaos, raging factions, and personal machines.

Responsibility for party support rests upon the taxpayers of the nation whose interests are served. Many bills have been before Congress from year to year to provide that sort of aid. I do not favor, however, direct grants from the Treasury, because such support would eliminate the great importance to party vitality of voluntary giving. The alternative is to maintain the responsibility on the parties and their workers to collect directly from those who are in sympathy with one or another of the parties, but to make such collections easier by the inducement of some sort of tax credit or allowable deductions from taxable income.

Among all the proposals for facilitating contributions, I believe that the following would be the best and the fairest to both parties. It would permit a tax credit for contributions up to ten dollars, providing the total contribution would be not less than twenty dollars. This would provide an inducement to the donor but would also require him to make an out-of-pocket gift to the party of his choice of at least an equal amount. It would also put the responsibility on the party to make the solicitations.

Beyond that, there should be a provision for contributions up to a larger amount, say up to three thousand dollars, which could be deducted from income just as charitable contributions are allowable now.

Such contributions would be to specified party authorities, perhaps the two national committees. They would apply only to the payment of expenses incident to primaries and elections for Federal offices. Strict accounting should be required, and each donor should receive a receipt which could be attached to his income tax return.

My purpose in limiting the system to the Federal level is that the responsibility for accounting for the funds would be centralized in two authorities and not scattered among the many state and local units of the parties. However, state and local party units would benefit from such a plan because they could then keep the money they collect in voluntary contributions. Under present practice some of it has to be given to the Federal party authorities.

The amount which would be lost in Federal revenue by such a system would be negligible. If we can spend many billions in aiding foreign countries to grope their way to free institutions, certainly a few million can be afforded to keep our own two-party system alive, healthy, and honest.

CHAPTER 27

The Essentials of Organization

ONE of the least known items of Abraham Lincoln's wisdom is a prescription he once wrote for party success:

The whole state must be so well organized that every Whig can be brought to the polls. So divide the county into small districts and in each appoint a committee. Make a perfect list of the voters and ascertain with certainty for whom they will vote. . . . Keep a constant watch on the doubtful voters and have them talked to by those in whom they have the most confidence. . . . On election days see that every Whig is brought to the polls.

Organization, more often than not, means success or failure in party operations. Issues may be solid. Candidates may be attractive. But when organization operates only periodically before elections, when it falls down in its recruiting and training of workers, when it falters in taking the offensive against its political opponents, when it does not sustain even the interest of its own workers, it must suffer inevitable, though unnecessary, losses. It is an army of irregular "summer soldiers."

The Republican Party as an organization is out-registered in many states. On a showdown in 1960 it could not deliver the vote to defeat the Democratic national ticket, supported as it is by powerful auxiliaries outside that party. Foremost among these groups are the AFL-CIO Committee on Political Education (COPE); public-power groups; the ADA; and other organizations. The GOP cannot expect this liberal Democratic combination to weaken in the long pull ahead. It now must face a new, powerfully organized force in the Democratic Party. There is a Kennedy machine, directed by two and possibly three Kennedy brothers, backed by enormous Federal patronage.

Better organization, then, is the paramount need of the GOP. Poor organization lost almost all decisive states in 1960. Replies to a questionnaire submitted to state chairmen by the Chairman of the Republican National Committee, William E. Miller, are most significant. Only eleven of the forty-five state chairmen who replied gave full time to their party duties. Of these, only seven received a salary for their labors. Among the forty-five responding, thirty-nine have permanent headquarters with at least one salaried person, and thirty-one have at least one paid staff member with executive rather than purely clerical duties. At least fourteen state Republican organizations have no headquarters on a permanent basis.

The Republican Party over nearly all of the nation is most inadequately staffed. In considering this deficiency in organization, especially in the Congressional districts, it should be noted that organized labor's Committee on Political Education alone uses a host of paid, professional labor organizers in *every* political campaign.

When COPE entered campaign operations in Michigan, at the very least several hundred paid organizers from the unions were thrown into politics. The Republican Party in Michigan had only a few paid, professional organizers. It is no mystery why Michigan became a stronghold of the Democratic Party.

Considered nationally, this disparity between the professional forces available to the two parties, largely due to labor unions' participation in politics, spells the difference in strength between the parties.

So it was in 1960. States vital to the Kennedy-Johnson ticket were swung by efficiently organized minority groups, mostly in the cities. Where Nixon-Lodge won it was through effective efforts by state, city, and county organizations.

In 1960 the greatest weakness of the Republican Party was in the urban centers of the country. While a record-breaking sixty-nine million voters went to the polls in that year, fewer than twelve thousand actually determined the result.

According to Dr. William B. Prendergast, Research Director of the Republican National Committee, the sharpest reversal of voting behavior from the election of 1956 appeared among city dwellers and suburbanites. Dr. Prendergast makes these points:

Chronic Republican weakness again centered on the big cities in the industrial and populous Northeast: on Detroit, Philadelphia, Newark, Boston, New York, Chicago, St. Louis, Pittsburgh, Cleveland and Baltimore. The margins by which Kennedy carried the states of New York, Pennsylvania, Michigan, Illinois, Minnesota, Missouri, Maryland and New Jersey with 173 electoral votes were provided by one large city in each state. In the 13 cities of over 300,000 inhabitants located in these 8 states, Kennedy picked up pluralities of almost 2½ million votes.

Nixon carried only Columbus and Indianapolis of the 20 cities of over 300,000 which lie inside the northeastern quarter of the U. S. In only 5 others did he receive as much as 40–50% of the vote: in Cincinnati, Kansas City (Mo.), Minneapolis, Rochester and Toledo.

In Southern and Western cities, by contrast, Nixon ran well. He carried 7 of the 11 largest Western cities and 5 of 9 Southern big cities. Only in New Orleans did he poll lower than 42% in the big cities of the South.

Fully recognizing the weakness of Republican organizations in the urban centers in 1960, Chairman Thruston Morton early in 1961 appointed a Committee on Big City Politics. The report of this committee was submitted by its chairman, Ray C. Bliss, to the new National Chairman, William E. Miller, in January, 1962.

Bliss's group spent eight months studying what happened in the big cities in 1960, analyzing ways to cut down metropolitan losses, and examining the mechanics and techniques of campaigning in urban centers. The Bliss report noted that in state after state—monotonously—Nixon came up to the big city lines with a thumping lead, only barely to lose it by margins piled up by Democratic organizations and labor's COPE. Nixon lost Pennsylvania in the precincts of Philadelphia, Michigan in Detroit, Illinois in Chicago, and Missouri in St. Louis—a total of 102 electoral votes in these four states alone.

The Bliss report makes clear that Republican organizations in many big cities have lacked adequate resources in funds and manpower to compete with well-financed and heavily manned ward and precinct organizations available to Democratic leaders through COPE and local political patronage. In twenty-five cities with a population of twenty-five million, the Republicans had only thirty-seven full-time paid workers. Of thirty-four city organizations responding to the survey, twenty-four answered that even on election day all their precincts had not been fully manned in 1960; only eighteen reported a full-time, paid executive officer of any kind; only three a full-time, paid finance official.

In 1960, only 1,100 of Philadelphia's 1,615 precincts were manned by the Republican Party. Nixon received 31.9 per cent of the vote. A year later, in the statewide race for the state supreme court the number of precincts manned climbed to 1,350. The Republican candidate received 43.5 per cent. Better precinct work contributed to the better showing.

The Bliss report recommended model organizations for a city or county committee, full-time professional staffs, year-round precinct organization, no matter how small, precinct training programs, and that worker recognition should be given wide attention and application.

The name of Ray C. Bliss has become well known in national politics because of the outstanding record which he achieved in Ohio in the 1960 election. Ohio was carried by the Republican ticket that year by the largest of any state Republican majority. Bliss is chairman of the Ohio State Central Committee and is also a member of the Republican National Committee from his state. His operation in Ohio in 1960 deserves a somewhat detailed description, since it might serve as a model for many other states.

In the 1958 election in Ohio the labor unions fought with money and manpower to defeat a right-to-work amendment. A number of unfavorable developments contrived to make the year a difficult one for Republicans even without that issue.

In that year, despite the protests of experienced politicians, including Senator John W. Bricker and Bliss, a segment of businessmen in Ohio put right-to-work on the ballot by referendum. Labor had long anticipated this and had mobilized its professional forces and gathered money to meet the imagined threat to its existence. The result was a tremendous defeat for the amendment, which reacted disastrously upon Republican candidates. The party was shattered. It lost all along the line—the United States senatorship, the governorship, and the legislature. Republican congressmen lost hitherto safe seats. The total vote was close to 2.4 million as against 1.8 million in 1950, the year union leaders put forth great efforts to defeat Senator Robert Taft. The difference was the Democratic vote. Democratic labor was given a "live issue." Right-to-work proponents failed to arouse support.

However, State Chairman Bliss moved into the wreckage the next day. In the period between the election of 1958 and the beginning of the Presidential campaign in 1960 he reorganized the party over the state. He inspired county chairmen, women's groups, finance chiefs, business leaders, and volunteer workers with his objective to carry the state for the national ticket, to regain control of the legislature, to hold Congressional districts with precarious Republican majorities, to win back others from the Democrats, and to prevail in state and county offices.

Bliss maintained a staff of trained field men to work in key counties and a speakers' bureau. TV programming was carefully employed. "Lunch-and-Learn" programs were held to instruct volunteers. It is most important to note that Bliss saved most of his funds in 1960 for the months of October and November. By contrast, there were major states in which the GOP spent so much in August and September that, despite effective, attractive candidates on the ballot, the organizations were underfinanced and exhausted in the final weeks of the campaign.

Bliss is an "organizing" chairman, not a "speaking" chairman. He explains that his forte is organizational work, that he had to be at his headquarters to keep his staff functioning at top efficiency and to be in a position to make the right decisions at the right time. "There's a tremendous investment there," he says.

Had Bliss not been in his office, the result in Ohio would not have been so impressive. By seeing everything of importance that came in, by making decisions, and by maintaining an alert staff he achieved astonishing success.

In his office on High Street, Columbus, he decided that there was a "soft Kennedy feeling" among 5 or 6 per cent of those expected to vote for Kennedy. His personal "postcard poll" helped him in arriving at a decision to move with speed on this intelligence late in the campaign. He tied up every available television station in the state for an hour after the immensely popular Cleveland Browns' football game, on a Sunday afternoon "when viewers were sitting around without too much to do." Truth Squad material was used. Then he placed full-page ads in every big-city daily in Ohio on Thursday and Friday mornings, Saturday afternoon and Monday. This action, he feels, paid big dividends: "There's a case where if I'd been on the road the decisions wouldn't have been made."

Bliss uses conferences to great advantage. Not that he thinks a great deal of knowledge can be conveyed, but that interest and concern can be generated. Periodically, county chairmen are given a broad picture of areas of weakness and areas of strength.

They are told what help they will get from the state headquarters and what they are expected to do.

The proof that better organization won in Ohio is offered by a comparison with Michigan. The populations of the two states are not dissimilar, although that of Ohio is larger. Michigan's largest center is Detroit. But Ohio has Cleveland and Cincinnati and Columbus and a number of other sizable urban centers. In both states industry is heavily unionized and in both there are large racial minorities. But Ohio was carried by Nixon by 274,000, while Kennedy carried Michigan by 67,000.

Superior organized Republican effort made the difference.

CHAPTER 28

Professionalism and Auxiliaries

POLITICS is a venerable art. As a profession it goes back to ancient times. It is not a science, although some scientific methods are applicable. It is not without significance that our greatest classic master of politics, Aristotle, was the son of a surgeon whom the young philosopher assisted in his professional duties. His writings show that there is in politics a body of knowledge that requires training and study.

But now, in a period when new professional specialties are emerging on every side, the "professional politician" is still regarded with condescension, as a lowly sort of fellow who cannot make a living at anything else. This is the more surprising when it is considered that those who have enjoyed most success in political and official life have had long and arduous training for the practice of the art. Witness Jefferson, Lincoln, Coolidge, the two Roosevelts, Truman, Nixon, and Kennedy.

Practice is essential to the training of the political organizer, just as it is in medicine and engineering. But there is also a body of knowledge which can be transmitted by education. An imperative need in strengthening our two-party system is that this training be recognized, systematized, and actively promoted. The Republican Party, which has no such professional help as the political unions are lending the Democrats, should have schools specifically designed to educate and train professional political organizers. This education cannot be imparted by the halfway methods of short conferences and round tables. It should provide training over a period of weeks, or preferably months.

Some of the party funds might well go toward establishing a Republican Academy which could handle groups or classes of about fifty. Possibly the faculty could be recruited from academic life as well as from other professions—political and business management, advertising, public relations, journalism, and law. Promising men and women, interested in a career in politics, might pay a fee and expenses while attending. Or possibly the national, state, and county organizations might assume this expense for training of selected individuals.

Instruction should include the wide range of political fundamentals and activities which would turn out informed, well-rounded organization people. Techniques of managing campaigns from county and city up to national offices, fund-raising at various levels, legal aspects of political activity, filing and maintaining records, research techniques, use of media, handling issues, advertising and promotion, public speaking, writing releases, relations with the press, uses of contacts and polls, and other topics might be given treatment.

Of course, as is now the case for conferences and workshops, special speakers from many fields could be brought in for lectures and question-and-answer periods.

Certificates of graduation should testify to a high quality in aptitude and a sound foundation in knowledge. Persons with this training should be employed throughout the levels of the party.

One area where more professionalism is needed is that of the marginal Congressional district. With two hundred or more trained, paid, full-time political organizers and managers for deployment in large communities and Congressional districts, the Republicans might well equate and surpass the advantage now possessed by the Democrats through the political arms of the unions. Nothing less can more certainly achieve what the oft defeated Republican Party is seeking. No symphony of words; no campaign fund, however lush; no advertising campaign; no "virile young candidates" can be sufficient to turn the balance without able, professional management. A party faith is necessary, it is true, and better candidates can help greatly. But trained, professional men and women are indispensable.

While every conservative is urged to work within the Republican Party and thus to strengthen it, there are ways and means of providing help for the party through auxiliary organizations. This can be especially important in the large urban centers. As yet great numbers of Americans whose inclinations and interests run counter to the programs of the liberal Democrats for one reason or another are unwilling or unable to participate actively in Republican Party activities. They can, however, serve in auxiliaries, and party regulars should recognize the potential influence of such groups. Roosevelt and Flynn and Democratic strategists recognized the importance of Democratic auxiliaries. COPE is, in fact, such an auxiliary.

The creation of an auxiliary may begin with the efforts of one or a few citizens. A small group may then invite larger numbers of interested citizens to join them. The target may be a group large enough to encompass a large urban area. It may limit itself to a single Congressional district, a county, or merely a neighborhood.

The first important step to take when such a group is planned is to make a friendly contact with the official Republican Party organization in the area. The purpose of an auxiliary is to help and not supplant or compete with the legally constituted party. It should make the fact abundantly clear that while it must collect funds for its purposes, it is not going to seek contributions to which the party organization is entitled. The best way to manifest its good faith is to contribute, so far as it can, to the funds of the party organization. It should also permit the regular organization leaders to reap the benefits of publicity. Never should a member or leader of an auxiliary group forget that these regulars have carried the heavy burden of party organization through many campaigns while others have indulged in political apathy. The more I have learned of practical local politics, the more I respect those hardy perennials who have scorned delights and lived laborious days and nights in the service of a party. They have proved their willingness to toil on through years of party defeat and disaster. Once you see at first hand how difficult it is to induce good candidate material to offer itself and how niggardly the "best people" are with their time and money, your admiration is aroused for these regulars. If there are honors to be enjoyed and flowers to be gathered in the arid fields of practical politics, the regulars should be allowed them.

The sort of auxiliary which I am discussing is not a nonpartisan group. It should be a Republican group dedicated to the success of Republican candidates and Republican causes. Such an auxiliary can best be illustrated by describing two examples.

The first was created in 1946 in one of the Congressional districts in a large Midwestern city. The head of a medium-sized manufacturing company called together a number of fellow Republican businessmen to defeat a man who they believed had misrepresented the district in Congress. This small group pooled brains, energy, and money to form a much larger group which applied effective managerial methods in recruiting volunteers, in publicizing a selected candidate, and in getting out a sympathetic vote for him. A large majority for the incumbent in 1944 was turned into a whacking majority for the new man in 1946. This group then extended its influence and methods into other Congressional districts and into campaigns for the state legislature. The organization still operates. Its operations are not secret, but it has never taken a name and it shuns public notice.

The Republican Associates of Los Angeles County was created by a number of leading citizens in that county in 1952 and has since been in operation continuously. It includes in its membership more than five thousand business and professional men and women. It conducts year-round research and volunteer training and formulates programs and policies designed to promote the election of Republican candidates. It does not select the candidates. That is the legal responsibility of the regular Republican organization in the county. But as its membership has grown year after year, it has provided a number of important services to the party in campaigns.

In 1960 the Republican Associates recruited and trained speakers for the Republican county committee and also for the Southern California speakers' bureau of the state committee; it provided research assistance for Republican candidates in the county; it trained volunteers for assignments by the county committee. By election day 1960 the Republican Associates had more than four thousand such volunteers in the field. When national leaders of the party came to Los Angeles County, the Republican Associates provided executive talent to act as advance men in preparing for their meetings.

Between campaigns the Republican Associates staff continues its research and issues publications. It also holds general membership luncheons.

At the present time the influence of the Republican Associates is being felt in other centers in the state of California. In San Francisco there is a group called the Republican Alliance, built on much the same plan as the Los Angeles organization.

A basic responsibility of the Republican National Committee should be to assist in creating such organizations in many of the other urban centers of the country. If that could be done in not more than thirty or forty such centers, the political complexion of the nation might well be changed.

CHAPTER 29

Republicanism and the Business Community

THE business community means all of those individuals
who produce the material means of life—those who work with
their hands, those who plan and manage, and those who invest.
Since many of those are also consumers, there should be no essential conflict between those who consume and those who produce.
Economic life is a "seamless web." To tear one part is to distort
the whole.

Business, therefore, is almost all of us—wage-earners, farmers,
small proprietors, managers, investors, and scientists. All are
concerned with the vast range of government intervention in economic life and with what government does about and with our
money. Therefore, all bear a responsibility for that political action
which determines who shall be entrusted with government and
with the policies which government adopts.

As a national organization the Republican Party must appeal
to all the interests which make up the business community. This
includes the rank and file wage-earners, union and nonunion.
Apparently, the leaders of the politically oriented unions have
permitted themselves to become dedicated adjuncts of the liberal
Democratic Party. This is shown in every speech they make, in
their direction of the activities of their political agency, COPE,
and in every issue of the AFL-CIO *News*. Every issue of that pub-

lication is replete with attacks on the Republican Party and with arguments for the policies of the liberal Democrats.

This attitude of the leaders of these unions, however, is no reason why the Republicans should not carry on efforts to reach the rank and file of union members. They enjoy the political freedom which is accorded to all citizens. A large number conceive their political preference to be quite unrelated to their interests in issues in collective bargaining and other services of the union. They cherish their freedom of choice in elections. They resent bossism, even by their union leaders.

Also, their economic status has moved them up in the middle incomes. They share the same concerns in sound and economical government policies as management executives and small proprietors. They are investors, often in the companies in which they work. They are in every sense "capitalists" now. They should be conservative, for they have so much more to conserve. For these reasons and many others, the Republican Party deserves its full share of the votes of wage-earners, union and nonunion alike.

In the cities and growing suburban areas, workers, who once voted Democratic, live close to Republican neighbors. They own similar homes or occupy similar apartments. They may play on the same golf courses, belong to the same lodges and fraternities, attend the same churches, and participate in community affairs generally. Their wives confront the same problems as do Republican women in these neighborhoods—the same index of living costs and concern over financial matters. They must bear the same debilitating effects of taxation and inflation. Their prospects of a secure retirement are equally influenced by the gradual destruction of the value of savings and of their husbands' retirement benefits.

In 1956 the Republican National Committee established a rank and file labor division under Campaign Director Robert Humphreys with a director and a staff of four field men, all with union backgrounds. These field men encouraged state committees to set up similar divisions to work in the counties, cities, and towns. A number of states established exceptionally effective programs. As Humphreys explains:

Our field men stayed in the field almost 100 per cent of the time working at the state and local levels with local field men or organizers. The organizational plan was very simple: just make it possible for a union member to join a Republican rank and file committee. Unionists and their wives were invited to do organizational work, wear buttons, and carry on the word-of-mouth activity among their fellow union workers.

The use of the words "rank and file" was chosen deliberately, not because we intended to confine ourselves to rank and file unionists but because we wanted the heavy emphasis on them and because we knew we had no chance to get any of the international labor presidents in our camp and very few state leaders. We did not want a "front" committee of stuffed-shirt labor leaders who would meet maybe once during the campaign and issue a statement.

Another part of the plan provided that Republican organizations find unionists who could do organizational work. Republican organizations around the country found that many men belonging to unions were precinct workers or county committeemen. In New Jersey one out of five of 7,500 county committeemen were dues-paying unionists. In New York State the unionists accounted for approximately 17 per cent of New York's 25,000 county committeemen. Other areas had the same experience. In other words, it was discovered that many unionists who were Republican carried on their party role as plain citizens, not as unionists. Many had been reluctant to become identified for fear of retaliation, but in 1956 they shed this type of fear.

In 1956, 43 per cent of the wage-earners voted for the Republican candidate for President. It is probable that in 1960 a very considerable number of union members voted for Nixon. The union leaders who fought so hard against the re-election of Senator Taft in Ohio in 1950 discovered that they could not control the votes of their members. Taft won all the industrial counties because he carried his message to workers as Americans interested in sound principles of government, not merely members of unions. It would be a mistake for Democrats or the Democratic union leaders to consider that they have a monopoly of union members' votes. The Republican Party can capture a larger and larger percentage of the support of wage-earners, union and nonunion.

It is equally important to persuade managers and investors to take an active part in political activities at every level, especially in the communities in which they live.

For many years there existed what I have called "the business-man's complex." This seems to have crept into the minds of managers and owners many years ago at a time when the Progressive movement quite properly attacked the close alliance between them and the Republican Party. The "image" then created of the Republican Party as an agent of "big business" has had a sort of immortality largely because Democratic demagogues have harped on it for so long. To shake off this "image" has been the declared purpose of responsible Republican leaders. This can be accomplished not by vying with liberals in offering lavish promises. Rather, it can be accomplished by a broad appeal based upon the common interests of all members of the economic community.

But the earlier attacks upon business "interests" have had a serious effect upon leaders of business. Their reaction has been profound and unfortunate. Men of large corporate affairs became obsessed with the feeling that their activity in politics, even their legitimate support of candidates of their choice, would be the "kiss of death." The head of one of the largest of American corporations once told me that he would not be caught participating in politics "because people don't like me." Collateral with this fear of censure there developed among business managers the belief that their talents were wholly unsuited to the tasks of political organization. It was believed that "businessmen make incompetent politicians."

Gradually, however, these impressions have diminished. There is no reason why a good employer should not be welcomed as a participant and adviser in the complexities of political life. The public which invests millions because of its faith in a company's product should not distrust those who manage that company. In community affairs such individuals are welcomed and their talents are used. And after all, politics is a community matter, too.

Moreover, as Lord Woolton's amazing success as a political manager in Britain after a life in business shows, the managerial talents of business are, with slight modifications, exactly what are needed in party affairs.

Within the past ten years a very considerable change has taken place in the attitude of business management toward politics. There is a growing realization that with government entwined so closely with the economic system, the distinction between private and public interests is diminishing. Business managers—and this is most important—are growing to realize that as citizens and members of the community they have a moral obligation to participate in political affairs. Corporations which hitherto have had a rule that no executive, no matter how low in the hierarchy, should participate in politics have relaxed and have encouraged their management employees to participate in politics.

Large trade associations have established training courses in practical politics for business executives. The Chamber of Commerce of the United States, under the leadership of a committee headed by Arthur H. Motley, a dynamic publisher, with membership drawn from presidents and other officers of corporations, lawyers, and others, worked prodigiously to interest business managers in politics. The Chamber's staff set to work to prepare material on practical politics for educational purposes. The result has been a series of manuals comprising an "action course in practical politics," used in the training of business employees, executives, and others at the community level. The courses are designed "to give businessmen and others information to show them how they can help to elect qualified candidates to office—local, state, and national." The Chamber is actively promoting the use of these courses, which include a practical discussion leader's manual and a set of eight "how-to-do-it" pamphlets and other material.

The political programs of the Chamber are aimed at the community level. They recognize the great potential in the young or junior management people. And the Chamber provides direction to many corporations that are developing programs of their own.

Already, vigorous programs have turned out thousands of men and women trained in the fundamentals of political action. Many who have participated in those programs are working in the two-party system. Some are block workers; others, committeemen and committeewomen. A few hold political office as a consequence of their recent participation.

Graduates should receive follow-up information and advice. In some instances the Republican Party in their communities has not shown enough interest in these newcomers, has even discouraged their political activity. In this case, there is something seriously wrong with the local party. For the imperative need in the Republican Party is executive talent.

In conclusion, it is most essential to emphasize that this renewed activity in politics by business executives and white-collar workers should be wholly divorced from the specific interests of the corporation as such. These people enter the political arena, not as members of a specific economic interest, but as citizens performing their duty in the party of their choice. They must under no circumstances portray themselves as antilabor or antiunion. To do so would reopen the angry scars of a generation ago and contribute to the creation of a class conflict between the parties. Management and union membership have a common stake in better government, sound economic policies, and individual liberty.

CHAPTER 30

Women, a Neglected Asset

IN 1960, shortly after the Republican convention in Chicago, I wrote the following comment in an article in *Newsweek:*

The elaborate plans for the Republican convention provided several functions of a supposedly feminine nature for the wives of the statesmen. These were teas, style shows, and the like for Mrs. Eisenhower, Mrs. Nixon, and others. Every effort seemed to be made to draw the attention of women from such presumably abstract subjects as budgets, foreign affairs, government regulation of labor and business, and economic growth. Such serious matters the perspiring gentlemen of the convention seemed to regard as within their sole province and understanding.

Most Republicans never seem to realize that women are not merely "ladies." They hold to a deep Victorian belief that women are to be seen and not heard, entertained rather than consulted.

In that failure to understand that women have brains, education, judgment, a close understanding of every-day affairs, and an infinite capacity for organization work, the Republican Party is neglecting a most vital asset for success at the polls. Perhaps that out-dated concept that women's place is in the home is one of the major reasons why Republicans have failed to get enough votes to win elections.

Now, two years later, I have no reason to modify that criticism. It is true, as I was reminded in letters after the article was published, that the Republican National Committee in Washington has a most active and efficient women's division. Also, there are equally active and devoted women's organizations in many of the states and local communities. And throughout the various organizations in the Republican Party, from the National Committee down, there are committeewomen and co-chairmen. But still there is a failure to use the potential of women to anything like the extent that is necessary.

Through long tradition the significant decisions in the party are made by men. The various women's groups were created to effectuate those decisions in the processes of administration.

In the many meetings of trade associations which I have attended over the years, I have noted that while the businessmen were considering how they could take a more effective part in political life, the wives were generally relegated to style shows or exclusively feminine luncheons. This lack of comprehension that women are able to understand the profundities of political life, so ingrained in men generally, is hard to break through.

That is not true in the immensely efficient operations of the labor unions in politics. Women bear the major part of the job of securing full registration and of getting out the vote. They are also skilled in presenting the arguments to individuals and groups.

In England, women are extremely active and influential in the new Conservative Party.

The concept which has lingered so long among men—that women are less interested in and capable of understanding political issues and problems—is simply not true. I have particular qualification to offer evidence on that subject. For more than thirty years in college and university teaching I had hundreds of women students in classes in politics and government. Compared with the men studying the same subjects and in the same classes, the women worked harder, read more, and were invariably better qualified to understand the psychological subtleties of politics. They also earned grades running about 20 per cent higher.

Both in academic life and in the business of practical politics women resent being treated as a separate species. They want to share the responsibilities of politics on equal terms with men.

I once noted, in speaking to a group of women workers in politics, that in three respects women are more useful in a campaign. They have emotion, devotion, and time.

Long ago, in his play *What Every Woman Knows,* James M. Barrie very perceptively portrayed the emotional sophistication of a character called Maggie, who was able to make a success of her dour, uninspired husband in British politics. When he left her he lost his standing in the Parliamentary party. She had what is called "political sense," a value which is impossible to define except to say that unless one has it, he had better not try a political career.

The woman worker in politics labors with complete devotion. In the City of New York, a professional political worker, Alice Ruth Miller, once said that the three essentials in a political campaign were "toil, sweat, and volunteers." Getting a lethargic electorate to the polls requires a lot of prosaic labor, endless house calls, telephoning, stuffing envelopes, and generally keeping store at headquarters. Here women seldom complain. They realize that without this toil there can be no success. Another notable woman political worker complained that in the Republican Party "there are too many chiefs and not enough Indians."

On one occasion, when I was teaching, I asked the greatest woman politician of her time, the late Ruth Hanna McCormick Simms, to speak before a class of women students. She told of her experience working as a young girl with her father, Mark Hanna, when he was promoting the candidacy of William McKinley for President. She told also of her life in Illinois politics, in which she had so important a part in electing her husband, Medill McCormick, United States Senator. She described her own successful campaign for congressman-at-large from Illinois, and her subsequent experiences in politics in New Mexico. At the end of the lecture, a young woman asked her, "What is the greatest asset in a successful politician?" She replied, "Good manners." By this she meant something far more important than observing the rules of etiquette. She meant warm concern for the rights, convenience, and dignity of others; an agreeable manner which keeps the other fellow's interests in the foreground. Above all, political behavior means attention to many little things: "Let me first be faithful in those things that are least, then I also will be faithful in much."

These are assets that the Republican Party needs in the practical business of getting votes. And women can supply them in good measure.

I have noted that a third of the stock of American corporations is owned by "housewives and nonemployed, adult females." Their property interests in other areas are also immense. They have much to conserve. And it is not surprising that they are generally conservative. Their concern in the problems of international peace is almost passionate. They cherish the ideal of an orderly, economical government. They live closer to the problems of the consumer and are the first to detect the approach of inflation.

In 1950, in the British general election, the Labor government was in trouble when it was reported that wives of workers were beginning to question the management of the government. Some asked whether their husbands, devoted members of the Labor Party, would know how they themselves voted. The results indicated that many of the socialists found their votes cancelled by those of their wives. The women, as one of them remarked, were "fed up with socialist austerity."

The greater conservatism, and therefore the greater preference for the Republican Party, among women was shown vividly in a most important "market survey of potential voters," published by the Republican Associates of Los Angeles in 1960. This survey consisted of interviews with 2,308 eligible voters representative of 75 precincts in the county. The results showed conclusively that while women show a lower rate of voting, they are by conviction more conservative and more inclined to vote Republican than are men. No doubt, the reason why they fail to vote is that the party leaders neglect to make an effort to enlist their co-operation in campaigns.

There is nothing esoteric about the basic political issues which face the citizens of this country. They concern our posture toward international Communism—the capacity of our government to meet the threat—the prudence of that government in meeting its obligations without ruinous inflation, the necessity that government be kept close to the citizens whom it serves, the efficiency of government in meeting its daily tasks, and the limitations which must be fixed upon government welfare and subsidies. These issues our women are perfectly capable of understanding. In a political party their common sense, their idealism, and their capacity to contribute to its success in elections could be decisive. Those vested with official status in the Republican Party can ignore these assets at their own and the nation's peril.

PRINCIPLES AND POLICIES—
A PERSONAL APPRAISAL

AUTHOR'S NOTE

As the caption of this section indicates, the policies outlined in the chapters that follow are a purely personal appraisal. I disclaim any intention to ascribe them to the Republican Party or any of its candidates. In fact, two or three conservative individuals to whom I have shown these chapters have advised me to omit them entirely. Such specifications, they said, generate disagreement, even among those who would generally agree with the thesis of this book.

I appreciate all too well that a party and its candidates must consider many details in the context of changing circumstances. This is not mere expediency, so long as ultimate goals are not compromised.

The statesman in a campaign or in public office must consider timing and degree in what he proposes and supports.

However, by stating most of these suggestions in terms of principles, I hope I have contributed somewhat to the charting of a road away from contemporary liberalism. And so I submit them solely on my own as my personal choices of means toward sound national policies.

CHAPTER 31

The Good and Faithful Servant

GOVERNMENT—the several governments in our republic —touches us on all sides. As individuals a considerable part of our freedom of choice is preempted by the laws, regulations, and services of those governments, and these services and interven tions have been created for the most part by common consent. Most of them are part of the environment in which we live. Indeed, we could not very well live without them.

The liberal-conservative conflict as yet does not involve any change in the words of our Constitution. That, at least, has proved itself over the generations. No dictatorship or royalist authority threatens us. Nor, except in a small degree, are our religious differences introduced in our political life. Therefore, almost the entire area of our political differences relates to the extent to which government should serve us or intervene in our life as individuals. Those differences, however, involve us in a complex web of policy.

I have attempted to simplify these problems of choice in the plan of this book. It is based upon the concept of the primacy of the individual and the subservience of the government. It is a master-servant relationship applied to public policy.

We Americans have lived with our constitutional institutions at all levels long enough and have reached a sufficiently high level of intelligence, literacy, and common sense to be able to use them with safety and profit. Also Providence, our natural resources, and our enterprise have made us rich enough so that we can afford to spend a good deal in government services.

The practical problem before us is how to use government to the utmost limits of safety. Where those limits should be fixed is the problem of statesmen and citizens alike. The determination of them when applied to a multitude of human relationships is the root of the ideological division in our current American society. The liberal would place the burden of proof upon those who resist the enlargement of government authority. The conservatives ask for pertinent proof of the necessity and safety of such enlargements.

I believe that with a public opinion enlightened and stimulated by rational leadership, with a virile two-party system as the individual's means of control, and with agencies of communication and debate enjoying the privileges of free expression, all government—Federal, state, and local—can be entrusted with a wide range of responsibilities.

The conservative in accepting government service and intervention makes clear two fundamental conditions. He yields nothing to the liberal in his devotion to improvement and progress. Also, he does not limit his opposition to means alone. He recognizes that ends and means are inseparable.

The conservative, moreover, entertains a somewhat different evaluation of human nature. He recognizes the gradual perfectibility of man, but his respect for experience and tradition moves him to condition his expectations.

The obligation of statesmen and citizens should be to ask and answer a number of questions in meeting each specific issue:

1. Just what is the nature of the argument in proposing the specific program for a new Federal service or intervention?

2. What is the evidence of need for the new program?

3. So far as programs already in effect are concerned, have the original needs disappeared? In this we must bear in mind the

inertia which provides immortality to any specific activity of government. Progress involves continuous reconsideration and the possibility of repeal.

4. Are the alleged needs exaggerated or nonexistent?

5. When a demonstrated need is presented, what are the possibilities of meeting the problem by means other than direct Federal intervention?

6. Are there ways of meeting the need by private, co-operative means?

7. Can the need be met through some agency of government other than Federal?

8. If and when Federal intervention is proved to be the only means of meeting the need, how can the program be administered with the most efficiency and economy and the least possible limitation of individual liberty?

I summarize my indictment of liberalism in three counts: First, the assumption by the Federal government of services and interventions which limit unnecessarily the liberty of the individual and the operation of a free market; second, the assumption by the Federal government of responsibilities which have traditionally been left to the states and local government and which, because they are more effectively controlled by the states and local electorate, should remain there; third, the assumption by the Federal government of activities which should be the concern of private, co-operative agencies and institutions and individuals.

It will be noted that the foregoing specifications center upon the Federal government. They are matters of national concern. I recognize, of course, that state and local governments may and do impose upon individuals and private co-operative agencies and institutions unnecessary intrusions and restraints, but to account for these state and local activities would require another book.

It will be noted also that I have qualified my indictment by the words "unnecessarily," "more effectively," and "should be." The positions I take thus rest upon a personal judgment.

In the chapters which immediately follow I have made a selection of only a few among many of the issues which confront the Federal government and the American people. My consideration of them must necessarily be short and, I hope, pertinent. But they will serve as examples of how to deal with the essentials. These selections concern the protection of the individual, the measures which government must take in its intervention in economic life, the extent and limits of Federal contributions to personal welfare, the regulation of the money supply, and taxation.

Finally, I suggest with all emphasis that the Republican Party cannot provide an alternative to the people of this country by out-promising the liberal Democrats. In some instances it must, if it is to survive, present the hard truths to the electorate. But it may through a coherent explanation of the facts make it clear that its policies are a way—the only way—to the lasting welfare of the individual and the strength of the nation.

CHAPTER 32

The Protection of the Individual

THE responsibility imposed upon government to protect the individual presents a paradox. Individuals, "We, the people of the United States," create a government. Then they vest in that government the responsibility to protect themselves—against the government itself, other individuals, collections of individuals, and alien powers and influences.

In framing the Constitution in 1787, the authors were not unaware of the need for a specification of individual rights. But for the most part they assumed that the various states and their constitutions were adequate for that. Also, they were concerned with setting up a government to provide order and at the same time to make sure that the delineation of the respective rights of the nation and the states should be clearly defined. But no sooner had the document been presented to the country than there was a demand for a bill of rights as well. This was accomplished by the adoption of the first ten amendments.

The old problem, "Who shall guard the guardians?" (*Quis custodiet ipsos custodes?*) was largely vested in an independent judiciary. For the application of the Bill of Rights to the innumerable relationships among the individuals and between individuals and governments has always involved meticulous judicial definition.

Since the protection of the individual also involves collective groups of individuals called minorities, these must be protected from the majority. Somewhat related to this is the responsibility of the government to protect the collective majority, and the government itself, from combinations of minorities and individuals who seek to impair or destroy it. For a government is responsible for drawing the fine line between liberty and order.

In the vast literature on individual rights a number of observations of John Stuart Mill are models of common sense and clarity. In his essay "On Liberty" Mill goes far beyond the Benthamite school ("the greatest good to the greatest number") of which he was at first a member and spokesman:

The aim of patriots, therefore, was to set limits to the power which the ruler should be suffered to exercise over the community; and this limitation was what they meant by liberty. It was attempted in two ways. First by obtaining a recognition of certain immunities, called political liberties or rights, which it was a breach of duty in the ruler to infringe, and which if he did infringe specific resistance, or general rebellion, was held to be justifiable. A second and generally a later expedient was the establishment of constitutional checks, by which the consent of the community, or of a body of some sort, supposed to represent its interests, was made a necessary condition to some of the more important acts of the governing power.

Presumably Mill was thinking of such a functionary as a tribune of the Roman Republic. But he points out that the time was to come when individuals needed to be protected against not only the persons who constitute the governing power but the generality of the people themselves:

The "people" who exercise the power are not always the same people as those over whom it is exercised: and the "self government" spoken of is not the government of each, but of each by all the rest. The will of the people, moreover, practically means the will of the most numerous and most active part of the people; the majority, or those who succeed in making themselves accepted as the majority; the people, consequently, may desire to oppress a part of their number; and precautions are as much needed against this as against any other abuse of power.

It is when we seek to determine with some exactness what is practicable and safe in drawing the line between liberty and order that we encounter the greatest conflict of opinion. Mill recognizes a partial distinction for the age in which he lived. He points out that liberty to the individual must be limited in its exercise by one or some who would do harm to others. Further, he says that his doctrine is "meant to apply to human beings in the maturity of their faculties." It does not apply to children or to young people below the age fixed by law, "as that of manhood or womanhood." Despotism, he says, is legitimate when a government is dealing with barbarians.

Individual rights in the United States have successfully survived the greatest of all tests, the necessities of war. The government under President Lincoln found it necessary to contract individual liberty severely. But after the war had passed, the Supreme Court wisely liquidated those restrictions. In two world wars there were security restrictions. But since 1945, when Communist Russia precipitated a cold war, not only loosing upon the free nations in the West threats of military attack but also infesting these nations with a horde of spies and agitators, some of the security measures appropriate to a war status have been essential. Such security measures will of necessity remain so long as the Communist threat remains. But they have been and will continue to be subject to fierce debate among equally loyal Americans.

It is quite to be expected that there will be differences in opinion among us as to how seriously certain specific threats imperil the national safety. And since these internal threats involve secret operations by Americans influenced by Communists and Communism, there will be violent dispute as to methods of discovering and frustrating them.

However, it has been shown that throughout the 1930's, during the period immediately after World War II, and until the end of the war in Korea, there was laxness in the Administrations in power in security measures and too little apprehension by Presidents and Secretaries of State of the danger of internal subversion. This failure should not be imputed to the Federal Bureau of Investigation, which throughout has shown an extremely sensitive concern about internal subversion.

In the conduct of international affairs there were also grave mistakes in trusting the Soviet government in the summit meetings during the war and after, in the loss of China to Communism, in crippling, by our occupation measures, the capacity of Japan to protect itself, and in a failure to provide means for the defense of South Korea.

American Communists and fellow travelers had gotten into sensitive positions in government itself and into labor organizations and other private agencies, including educational institutions and the press.

Toward these internal dangers Congress at all times showed much greater concern than did the executive branch of the government. Also, the Supreme Court, in its anxiety to protect personal liberty, gravely underestimated during the 1950's the necessity for executive and legislative measures for protection.

Even in the Eisenhower Administration the Department of State, through its bureaucracy, certainly contributed to the Communist takeover in Cuba.

The history of the House Un-American Activities Committee and the various internal security subcommittees of the Senate indicated the great value of vigilance. Also, the votes in the House continuing the Un-American Activities Committee have indicated a greater popular concern than has been manifested by the executive departments and the Supreme Court.

Communism is not a philosophy which can be admitted as a legitimate shade of opinion within the area of debate in a free society. For its avowed purpose, as the agent of an alien and inimical foreign power, is to destroy free societies everywhere. Thus the Communist Party should be outlawed, and those who subscribe to the Communist philosophy should be considered as joining a movement conspiratorial in nature and subservient to an alien authority.

In maintaining liberty within a context of order there must be stern measures to protect government itself. For without government, no liberty can exist for anyone.

A final comment is necessary with regard to the protection of minorities. And I use the general issue of the rights of the Negro to illustrate my point. The Southern states which disagree with the rest of the states on this issue themselves constitute a minority. The Negroes within those states are a minority within that minority. Here we have the question of which of two minorities our government has a duty to protect.

In the field of industrial relations there is the issue of the right of a worker to join or not to join a union. The right of those workers who decline to join a union is arrayed against the right of the union to organize as a minority. There is also the right of the individual employer to enter into a closed shop agreement with a union. Here we have a very complex mixture of conflicting rights. The most difficult of problems as well as the most controversial arise when a right is arrayed against a right.

Indeed, there was a sharp division in the Supreme Court in interpreting the Taft-Hartley Act, which makes unlawful the use in politics of funds composed of union dues when a minority of those who contribute those funds oppose the candidate or party which the governing authorities of the union have decided to support. It was held by a minority of the Court that unions must operate "under a rule of the majority." In this instance, fortunately I believe, the majority of the Court held for the right of the individual as against the majority in his union, not only because no individual should be compelled to support a political cause which he opposes, but because to permit it would dangerously weaken the whole electoral process. Here an institution, free elections, was held to be paramount over the interest of the union.

These unresolved issues in our system of constitutional liberty, of which the foregoing are only a few examples, show our system to be in an imperfect state of development. That is to be expected since individual liberty has appeared so recently in civilization. Free institutions represent a quest, perhaps an unending quest, and not a goal.

CHAPTER 33

Guarding the Free Market

FREEDOM in the market place has been cherished among the traditions of Anglo-American civilization for more than two and a half centuries. The free market and the right to have and to hold private property have been and are regarded as essential to individual liberty. Government becomes the trustee to make sure that these principles be maintained inviolate.

To be sure, the intervention of government, even when such intervention is imposed by the full consent of the governed, is a limitation upon a completely free market. For complete freedom in economic life would mean a chaos in which very few individuals would have freedom at all.

While the concept of a free market should always be the guide in the making and enforcement of law, the issue is that minimum of restraint, aid, and control which will leave the largest possible scope for the exercise of individual initiative and effort and for reward.

The drawing of the boundary between economic freedom and government intervention becomes more and more difficult as economic interests become more complex. Ever since colonial days Americans have struggled with this issue. The American revolution was an assertion of the determination of Americans to resist the imposition of ill-considered directives of the parent government.

In the present context the claims of more than one interest are constantly in conflict. The fixing of a fair value of capital invested and of services performed—whether in manual labor or in judgment or skill—depends largely upon reconciling the predilections of the various individuals and groups concerned.

There is also interposed the interest of government itself. The ideal is a government holding the scales as an arbiter in economic affairs. The reality, too often, is a government operating as a positive political force. Government has the incentive of seeking more power. It is not a selfless agent, but something that creates claims of its own.

In my delineation of the problem and of the principles that should guide law-making and enforcement, I have arbitrarily limited myself to three interests in our economic life: ownership and management, labor, and agriculture.

Government Intervention in Ownership and Management

Here I specify only principles which will continue to be basic to all varying situations if we are to retain a free, competitive, healthy economy under certain restrictions imposed by government:

1.   Individual responsibility and voluntary co-operation, freely arrived at, are the characteristics of true economic liberty. They should be recognized as the ideal. Government can and should promote this ideal by suggestion and encouragement.

2.   To promote this ideal to the fullest extent, those entrusted with government should always be detached and judicial in their attitude. Political alliances with specific groups destroy this role of impartiality and by impairing the integrity of the executive and the Congress as courts of last resort invite class struggle and chaos.

3.   When individual and co-operative efforts fail and government assumes regulatory power, its function should be the making of rules generally prohibiting, not compelling. It is valid for gov-

ernment to tell a man not to do something against another man; it is not only impracticable but a denial of liberty to tell him exactly what he should do.

4. Government should not inject its will into matters that are within the realm of business judgment. It is not qualified to do that. The role of government as a judge, a mediator, and a regulator has been established over the centuries. Methods of operating in that capacity have been perfected. These are guidelines of principles, tested by experience and fixed in common and statute law.

On the other hand, in government administration of the activities generally known as business—manufacturing, buying, selling, lending, and the like—there is no body of skill or experience.

5. In all government regulation, the essential structure of our constitutional system should be respected. Federal regulation is appropriate only in matters that are truly interstate in character or are genuinely related to other Federal powers. Regulation, like other government processes, is at its best when those responsible are close to and familiar with the problem they seek to solve.

6. Since economic life is in a state of constant change, regulatory laws should frequently be reconsidered and revised. In fact, they may well be regarded as temporary invasions of economic liberty, subject to withdrawal when normal, free relations are restored.

7. All groups and interests should be held equally accountable to the public interest. Corporations, trade associations, and labor unions should be subject to the same or similar regulations.

8. The measure of the value of an economic system is its capacity to produce wealth; i.e., the goods that make for higher living standards, and the material means of human happiness. Government regulation should have this objective constantly before it. Thus, it should avoid unreasonably limiting by law the span of the individual's working life and hours. It should also restrict to a minimum the number of persons in nonproductive

government employment. It should not curb efficiency or check the flow of capital.

9.   In the conservation of natural resources, there are alluring temptations for the undue exploitation of government power. It is self-evident that some natural resources, especially those in the public domain, are limited in amount and are essential to the economy as a whole. Government, however, should generally act as a trustee of property belonging to the people, ultimately to be used by them under conditions of private ownership and development and not to be exploited for the enlargement of government power as such.

10.   The operation of a business by government is the deadly enemy of economic liberty. In competition with private business, government has overwhelmingly decisive advantages that lead to private ruin and state socialism.

11.   The test of all government intervention should be whether it truly contributes to the freedom, development, and security of the individual.

12.   Those who administer government should believe in a free economy. Former Prime Minister Attlee once said, "A socialist cannot hope to make a success of administering the capitalist system because he does not believe in it."

Liberties are indivisible. If economic liberty is not attained and held, the entire structure of principles, inherited and developed by experience, must fall.

Government Intervention in Labor Relations

Unlike corporations and other businesses, labor unions are a relatively recent factor in our political life. They were created because of the vast advantage enjoyed by an employing individual or corporation in dealing with a single worker. Since the proper function of government and law is to make sure that justice should prevail in all individual relations, it came to be recognized as necessary that government must correct this imbalance in bargaining power. Hence, government, with the support of public opinion, sought by law at first to protect the unions and then, by Federal statute and administrative machinery, actually to promote unionization.

But in the years since the Wagner Act was passed in 1935, the national and international unions have grown to great power. The workers of a great majority of the companies engaged in interstate and international commerce are almost completely organized. The unions have attained gigantic power in terms of membership, financial means, and political action. These unions are here to stay. Our political problem is to apply laws and regulations which will fit them into the context of a free society and the operations of a free, competitive economy. The problems involved are fourfold: To have orderly and free collective bargaining between two powers which are measurably equal. The public interest and convenience should be preserved. The consuming public should be protected against extortionate prices forced by employees and employers alike. And finally, the rights of individual workers, including union members, should be guaranteed against the coercions of the collective membership and also the leaders of the unions.

A few principles should prevail:

1. Government's efforts should be directed toward lessening, as far as possible, all intervention by government.

2. Legal compulsion by government should be designed for the sole purpose of protecting the freedom of all parties in industrial relationships. This principle should extend to the right of an employee to join or not to join a union.

3. Management, the individual employee, and the union should have open channels of intercommunication. Employees and unions should be free to express their views, suggestions, and complaints about policies of management. Management shares a responsibility to keep employees individually and collectively

informed of its policies and problems. However, there should be co-operation, not co-management.

4. The law should prohibit all strikes, boycotts, and picketing for reasons other than those directly affecting the company itself. Secondary and jurisdictional strikes should be outlawed.

5. Since foremen and other executive employees are a part of management, they should not be forced either by law or union coercion to bargain collectively with management.

6. Minimum wage legislation was originally designed to prevent the employment of persons at pay insufficient for a minimum standard of living. This original purpose should be adhered to. The trend now is to force all employers to pay average or prevailing wages. This is a grave injustice to management and workers alike.

7. The time has passed when government should, through its administrative agencies, actually assist in union organization. Monopolies of union labor, as well as ownership and management, should be subject to antimonopoly legislation on relatively equal terms. Exemptions hitherto enforced by law are outdated. There should be no industry-wide bargaining.

Government's Failure in Agriculture

It would be simple, and perhaps not far from the truth, to dispose of the problem of government in agriculture in this fashion: We now come to an approach to a free market in agriculture. The problem is insoluble. So much for the farm problem.

In the five years before the beginning of the war in Europe in 1914, American agriculture enjoyed a period of relative stability. There was little which needed government intervention. Even now, what is called "parity" is calculated on the basis of those years. But vast overproduction in the World War I years that followed left what we now call the farm problem. The 1920's saw growing distress on the farms. Many devices were proposed and some were adopted in those years. But the great depression only served to deepen the distress.

Then came Roosevelt's domestic allotment plan. This was held to be unconstitutional by the Supreme Court. Then Henry Wallace's soil conservation plan was adopted, in which government subsidies induced farmers to withdraw some acreage under the constitutionally permissible pretext that the idle land was being "conserved"—a word meaning a sort of renewal of its fertility. World War II provided a short period of relief. But the surpluses mounted as the world recovered. Then the Brannan Plan was announced. It was so absurd that even Congress rejected it. Under Eisenhower there was the soil bank, which failed.

As Nixon and Kennedy faced the campaign in 1960 it was necessary to say something constructive about agriculture. Nixon spoke in generalities, which the farmers apparently liked. For Nixon ran strong in the predominantly agricultural states. Kennedy had a sort of plan which he has since sought to have adopted. It seems at this moment to have pleased no one and to have provided no lightening of the drain on Federal funds.

The outlines of the problem can be grasped from the following facts:

1. The American farmer, today, feeds and clothes 25 persons. Ten years ago he fed and clothed 14.5 persons; 100 years ago it was only 4 persons.

2. Efficiency on the farm has gone up 72 per cent in the last ten years.

3. In the past fifteen years the yield of rice has increased by 58 per cent; corn yield has gone up 58 per cent; wheat yield has increased 90 per cent; and the potato yield has gone up a staggering 137 per cent.

4. Farm surpluses are up 151 per cent in the past ten years, and responsible and knowledgeable economists estimate that farmers will continue to increase their annual yield by nearly 6 per cent.

5. Gross income in the farm economy is up 18 per cent in the past ten years, yet trouble looms; expenses are up 37 per cent in the same ten years, and net income is down a frightening 14 per cent.

6. The United States Department of Agriculture now "manages" 24 per cent of the total farm production (only 17 of the 250-odd farm products are controlled) and this 24 per cent of the "managed" crops accounts for almost all of the $9 billion crop surplus now held in government storage bins.

The failure of government in the areas of these 17 crops under controls provides a ready contrast to the status of the more than 230 crops not under government control.

In the period from 1954 to 1959 the number of farms with gross sales of $10,000 or more annually increased by 36.2 per cent; the number of farms with gross annual sales of less than $10,000 dropped 30.8 per cent, and those farms with an annual gross sale of less than $2,500 dropped 39 per cent. The 1959 Census figures indicate that 54 per cent of the farms with gross sales of less than $2,500 are part-time units with operators who worked off the farm at least one hundred days each year or who had other family income. Another 24.7 per cent of farms in this income group are operated by people sixty-five years of age or over.

Thus the inexorable forces of nature, of supply and demand, and the powerful ally of scientific discovery are moving toward an ultimate solution which has baffled government so long. Farms are growing larger. Farmers are fewer by the year. And large corporate farming operations are taking over the production of food and fiber. An immense inducement for farmers to sell their land to larger units is the inflation in the price of land in the areas in which there have been large subsidies for nonproduction. In short, except as a romantic reminder of the earlier days, the family-sized farm is vanishing with the buffalo, the horse and buggy, and household industry.

The exodus of the individual proprietor is accompanied by no wails of distress. For the small owners are getting much more for their land than they could possibly gain through its cultivation.

Inevitably, these large areas under either individual or corporate ownership can be dealt with by government in the same manner in which it deals with manufacturing and other business enterprises.

In the interim, slowly diminishing subsidies will be necessary. To attempt to remove supports too soon would be ruinous and politically impossible.

CHAPTER 34

Principles of Personal Aid

Aɪᴅ to individuals unable to help themselves, or for whom no other form of aid is available or possible, is well established as one of the responsibilities in a free society. Those who hold this view predicate their position on the fact that the United States is rich enough and sufficiently humane to expect its various governments—Federal, state, and local—to make sure that no one falls below a reasonable minimum of personal security and well being. This can be done without either excessive government expenditures or restrictions upon personal liberty or the impairment of the moral fiber of our people.

There are principles, however, which should be observed at all levels of government:

1. The bestowal of government aid, except in cases of permanent incapacity, physical or mental, should always anticipate self-help. This has been the ideal of private welfare activities. The wisest social work administrator I ever knew made clear to his staff at all times that external help was a narcotic to be given with great care and as a temporary prop. The goal is to reestablish the individual or family in self-subsistence.

2. Aid beyond actual need is a deterrent to initiative and productive work. It should be the rule to maintain as many producing units in our economic life as is possible.

3. The test of need should be made for every grant of gov-

ernment aid at all levels, Federal, state and local. "Want" is something that the individual generates within himself. Need, so far as external help is concerned, must be determined by external authority, the authority which is providing the benefits. One of the favorite concepts of liberalism in government and elsewhere is that a test of need is somehow an affront to personal dignity, privacy, or what you will.

In the 1960 Presidential campaign the demagogic argument was presented by speakers including Messrs. Kennedy and Johnson that a needs test for medical aid for the aged would be a "pauper's oath." This ignored the plain fact that wholly aside from the moral and practical desirability of such a test, there is in fact a test of need in practically all of the welfare programs now in existence.

Unemployment compensation is to be paid only to those "willing and able to work," and under Federal regulations no state system can provide unemployment compensation except through public employment offices. OASI recipients must show that they are actually retired and that their income from work is not above a specified level. Age and other facts must be proved. The means test applies to Old-Age Assistance and other benefits.

Indeed, every income tax return is in essence a means test which invades privacy.

4. Personal aid, whether it be distributed by government, a private agency, or an individual, is not a "right." It is, in the best sense of the word, "charity." That this word has come to be regarded with derision and contempt is a sign of moral and spiritual decline. Charity is an encompassing concept, extending around the act of giving, compassion, and a sense of responsibility. It is sanctified in centuries-old tradition.

5. The administration of such aid should, so far as possible, be promoted by private means. The family's and relatives' responsibility comes first; the neighborhood comes next. Beyond that

come philanthropic agencies supported by individuals with the fine instinct of sharing.

6. When government participates in personal aid, its administration should be directed by an agency of the state close to the beneficiary. It should operate within the community and neighborhood. For the larger the unit of government which administers welfare, the greater the degree of impersonalized routine and red tape and, frequently, political advantage and private corruption.

7. When the Federal government grants direct personal aid, it should be only in cases of natural disaster, war emergency, or on a temporary basis, anticipating the rehabilitation or future contributions of those involved. With all Federal aid, direct or indirect, Federal control is constitutionally and morally mandatory.

The great majority of American welfare programs in the past have adhered to these seven principles.

Before tracing further the course of Federal aid, and in line with the foregoing seven principles, I suggest five objectives in any reform of the welfare programs which now absorb the largest part of the Federal expenditures, other than military, and whose operation requires the largest proportion of the Federal bureaucracy:

1. To make sure that no individual shall be in genuine need.

2. To be just both to the beneficiaries of aid and to the nation's taxpayers.

3. To enforce simplicity in administration, thus to prevent the further growth of the Federal bureaucracy and to reduce its present ranks.

4. To contribute to the improvement of Federal fiscal policies.

5. To restore responsibilities and appropriate tax sources to the states and local communities.

Reform of Old-Age, Survivors and Dependents Insurance

When President Roosevelt decided to emulate Britain in establishing a system of social security, I was still assisting him occasionally and unofficially. In the spring of 1934 he unfolded his ideas on the subject to me. He envisioned a system of partial insurance for old age. Regarding Federal sums to be granted to recipients in addition to their equities in the fund, he held to the principle of need. He specifically said that the tax collections for the trust fund should be invested in state and municipal bonds. He did not even consider at that time the thoroughly unsound, not to say fraudulent, idea of having the Federal government spend the social security tax receipts and deposit in the "trust" fund Federal bonds (or I.O.U.'s).

He commissioned me to write a message for him which was submitted to Congress on June 8, 1934. His concept of a social security system was to attain security

against the hazards and vicissitudes of life. . . . I am looking for a sound means which I can recommend to provide at once security against several of the great disturbing factors in life—especially those which relate to unemployment and old age. I believe that there should be a maximum of cooperation between the States and the Federal government. I believe that the funds necessary to provide this insurance should be raised by contributions rather than by an increase in general taxation. Above all, I believe that social insurance should be national in scope, although the several States should meet at least a large portion of management, leaving to the Federal government the responsibility of investing, maintaining and safeguarding the funds constituting the necessary insurance reserves.

The words "hazards" and "vicissitudes" were very carefully selected. To me in the drafting of the message, and to him in approving and delivering it, they meant demonstrated need. Congress, in passing the Act in 1935, had entirely different ideas, which have created the present monstrosity.

However, the word "insurance" does not appear in the original Act, for the logical reason that the system is not insurance. In fact, as I pointed out before, the Supreme Court in 1937 accepted the Justice Department's contention that the Act could "not be said to constitute a plan for compulsory insurance within the accepted meaning of the term 'insurance' " and ruled the Act to be constitutional under the general welfare clause.

I believe that we should return to that original concept of need. It is essential that there should be a radical overhauling of the system.

The concept which is held by so many prospective recipients, that OASI is "insurance," should be acknowledged for what it is—a fiction supported neither in the original law itself nor in the Supreme Court's interpretation of the law. The social security tax should be abandoned. Individuals having paid social security taxes should receive interest-bearing government bonds, payable at retirement age, either in a lump sum or in installments.

A fair subsistence allowance to all who have passed the retirement age should be paid out of funds collected by general taxation and appropriated yearly. Eligibility for such payments should be a demonstration of need, either in part or wholly, based upon a sworn statement of income from all sources. Such reports would be filed as income tax returns are now filed. Retirement age could be as it is, sixty-two for men and women. Special arrangements should be made vis-à-vis single and married persons.

Public Assistance Reform

The Federal government should turn over all public assistance programs to the states and local governments. Long-range bureaucratic control of such programs tends to be rigidly standardized, wasteful, and incompetent. Perhaps the shifting of this immense responsibility should be gradual to avoid personal hardships and also to ease the impact of support on state and local revenues.

An aim should be to loosen the Federal grasp on many tax sources now invaded by the Federal government. Since that will take some time to achieve, there should be consolidated grants-in-aid to states such as those described in Chapter 35.

Reform in Housing

Initially, provision for housing by our Federal government was limited to certain military necessities. Then, in the Administration of Franklin D. Roosevelt, the first and, at the time, the only step contemplated was the program of guaranteed mortgages. This was adopted largely to stimulate private housing and thus to activate the heavy industries and a measure of general economic recovery. It was in the late 1940's that the Federal government got actively into the business of housing.

In *The Death and Life of Great American Cities* Jane Jacobs states a powerful argument against government subsidized housing.[1] She points out that the creation of subsidized housing for the "low income" people sets aside in specific enclaves, certain classes in the population; that the divided responsibility for management between the Federal, state, and local authorities is inefficient; and that a concept that such housing is for "people who cannot be housed by private enterprise" is a way of destroying the entire structure of cities.

Quicker than the eye can see, the city as an organism has disappeared. It becomes, in theory, a static collection of sites for planting those sorted-out sets of statistics. From the beginning, the whole conception was irrelevant to the nature of the problem, irrelevant to the plain financial need of the people concerned, irrelevant to the needs and working of cities, irrelevant to the rest of the economic system, and even irrelevant to the meaning of home as it has evolved otherwise in our tradition.

The excuse given for building housing for people is that they cannot afford housing built by private enterprise. Since that is a matter of public assistance, the problem is not building houses

1 (New York: Random House, 1961), Chapter 17.

and managing them. Why not subsidize the income of those who need it through public assistance?

Removing government from the business of housing would eliminate a great windfall for the very rich who eagerly buy the tax-exempt bonds involved. It would also put a crimp in the speculative profits of slum owners who have done nothing to improve their property, but reap rich unearned profits from the sale of land to the government. It would greatly reduce the size of the Federal, state, and local bureaucracies. And it would encourage private building. For there is plenty of private capital to invest in housing if government interference were removed. Finally, with proper assessment practices established by local governments under the compulsion of state legislation, owners of land who are holding it for unearned profits would be forced to sell or improve their land by building.

There is no reason why the Federal system of guaranteed mortgages should not continue through the foreseeable future.

Education

The spurious character of the claims of need for Federal aid to education have caused the House of Representatives to reject the demand in successive years since 1949.

It remains here to indicate how school needs can be met without Federal aid and without the inevitable control which would be involved. In Roger A. Freeman's exhaustive study [2] of the way in which state and local governments can provide ample financing during the years until 1970, he makes a conclusive case for his contention that Federal financial aid is unnecessary. What is needed is a continuation of the adequate methods of financing schools which have prevailed in the past.

But the battle for local control is by no means conclusively won. In one way or another the Federal bureaucracy, backed by

[2] *Taxes for the Schools* (Washington, D.C.: The Institute for Social Science Research, 1960).

the National Education Association and the American Association of School Administrators, will continue in many indirect ways to guide the course of education. It rests with local communities, their school boards and their representatives, parents and citizens generally, to insist upon a number of basic changes in the schools—in their curricula and in the organization of the school year. It was a sad commentary on the quality of the present curricula that the schools had to be induced by Federal money provided in the National Defense Education Act to enlarge the offering of the schools in basic subjects. The demands of the future for more adequately educated people require the elimination of frills and inconsequential courses. The schools generally should remain in session more weeks and months in the year. Thus more use could be made of existing facilities and teachers could earn larger incomes by working as many weeks as individuals in private—and public—employment. It is mere habit and tradition that a teacher cannot work as long as an executive in a corporation or any other sort of white-collar worker. Citizens should throw the challenge to school administrators to modernize and strengthen their operation. It is not more money that is needed. It is more efficiency.

So far as higher education is concerned the problem is quite different. The drive of the Office of Education and the pressure groups is not to control higher education but rather education at lower levels. For colleges and universities have certain built-in protections. Faculties and trustees provide a barrier to Federal bureaucratic interference.

Regarding scholarships by the Federal government for individuals in colleges and universities, there is no demonstrated need.

The most vital of all protections of American institutions and individual liberty is and will continue to be decentralized public school education. This is an issue in which there can be no compromise.

CHAPTER 35

The States, Out of Bondage, Off the Dole

In his book, *The Sovereign States*, James Jackson Kilpatrick notes that in the Virginia Convention in 1788, which was debating the ratification of the new Constitution of the United States, a bitter argument took place between Patrick Henry and an aging and crippled Edmund Pendleton. Henry, with his customary violent eloquence, contended that under the proposed Constitution a grasping Federal government would seize the powers of the states one by one. Pendleton contended that "the two governments were established for different purposes, and act on different objects . . . they can no more clash than two parallel lines can meet." Henry was right. Pendleton's geometry didn't work.

But in these days, when the newspapers are full of news about state, city, and Federal budgets, we perceive no color or drama— only figures meaningless to most and confusing even to the expert.

But those figures, together with the various messages of governors reporting to their legislatures on the state of financial affairs, embody a threat to our constitutional system far more serious, for instance, than the barring of certain schools against Negro children. For in good time those schools will be open to all qualified scholars. But once the states are utterly dependent upon Federal funds to serve their people and in every state and local government the prying hands of Federal bureaucrats take over, the separate identity of Federal and state authority will be a fiction and the American people will have lost their mastery of their own affairs.

The progressive decay of the states is brought about by twin forces: the loss of their sources of taxation to the Federal octopus; and their acceptance of larger and more grants-in-aid.

Consider the stark reality of this expropriation. A central government, itself created by the original thirteen states, is telling the people of the states that they are not fit to tax and thus have the money to serve their collective interests. Uncle Sam is saying in effect: "I will take the money from your citizens and then give some back to you, telling you exactly what you can do with these 'gifts.' And to make sure that you don't make mistakes, we will loose upon you a horde of bureaucrats."

In submitting to this denial of their authority to spend their own money, the states and local communities have revealed an old human weakness. In the first place, the seizure of their tax sources has been gradual. And it has been accompanied by the suffocating aroma arising from "free" money from Washington. Under this influence their liberty has been dying happily. Indeed they have accustomed themselves to the habit of begging for the handouts.

When William H. Taft was President, Federal grants to the states amounted to only $3 million. By 1920 they were $33 million. In 1941, $836 million. In 1952, $4,176 million.

In his 1952 campaign Eisenhower took note of this growth and called for a return of tax sources to the states. But during his years in the White House grants-in-aid still continued their growth. In fiscal 1962, grants of all sorts, direct payments, trust fund expenditures, shared revenues, and the like reached the immense total of eight billion dollars.

A distinguished task force of the first Hoover Commission considered the danger of mounting grants-in-aid to states at some length. Its report, which met with vigorous opposition by some of its members, suggested that the following tax sources were appropriate for state and local taxation:

1. Sources widely and evenly distributed over the whole country.

2. Forms of business, wealth, and income of a nonmobile nature.

3. Sources in which receipts are obtained in connection with the regulation and enforcement of state laws (or local ordinances).

4. Sources related to special benefits, privileges, or protection received from the states or their subdivisions.

The sources which should be given to the Federal government should be:

1. Those which permit a high progression in taxation.

2. Sources highly concentrated in a few states.

3. Forms of business wealth and income of a highly mobile nature.

While no specific prescription can be laid down here for such a reallocation, a number of examples may be suggested. The Federal government should retain all customs duties, alcohol and tobacco excises, a flat rate on individual incomes much less than is now levied, the corporation income tax, and a few specific levies such as railroad payroll taxes for unemployment and retirement.

The states should exclusively have death and gift taxes, gasoline and lubricating-oil taxes, retail sales taxes, limited individual income taxes, business and severance taxes, and payroll taxes for unemployment benefits.

Local units should exclusively have property taxes, various admission and amusement taxes, retail sales taxes where states do not use them, and various licenses and fees.

While, as we have seen, grants-in-aid increased by billions

during his Administration, President Eisenhower remembered his campaign promise and after a vigorous speech before the Governors' Conference brought about the creation of the Commission on Intergovernmental Relations. A sizable number of liberals on this commission somewhat frustrated its efforts, but a good report was issued in 1955. But like the reports of the two Hoover Commissions, this one has been mostly ignored by Congress.

The serious nature of the seizure of tax sources and the practice of grants-in-aid is not alone measured in the gross amounts mentioned above. There is also the great number of grants earmarked for specific purposes. There are eighty of them. These involve a large number of controls by the Federal bureaucracy. Thus a horde of Federal bureaucrats invades state houses and city halls inspecting, checking, and dictating to local and state officials. I have heard many a governor complain bitterly about this interference. In some states there is opposition in the legislatures to "matching grants," which they do not consider necessary. But the lure of "free" money from Washington usually compels these state expenditures.

However, since so many of these programs have been established so long and the Federal government is so tenacious in holding all possible sources of revenue, I can see faint hope for a real allocation of tax sources in the next few years.

If we assume that grants-in-aid are here to stay for the foreseeable future, there are two alternatives which might not be so difficult to achieve.

The better of these would be to substitute for the miscellaneous specific grants a general grant to each state, without conditions as to what it shall be used for. A compromise version of this would be what are known as "consolidated grants." These would be earmarked only for certain general purposes, such as public health or highways.

These alternatives to tax source reallocation are considered in a study by President George C. S. Benson and Professor Harold F. McClelland of Claremont Men's College.[1]

Their study presents this argument in favor of general grants:

The most desirable substitute for existing grants would be a non-earmarked general grant to the states. As a substitute for existing specific grants it would at one stroke restore most of state autonomy and responsibility. It would eliminate the present unsatisfactory process by which the National Government impinges on state and local budgeting with little consideration of the needs of the individual state. It would restore to state and local officials the opportunity and responsibility to determine the policies of their own governments. It would renew opportunity for experimentation and adaptation of governmental programs to the needs of particular areas.

Objections would of course be raised. Some would maintain that national funds would be misused if the states were allowed to spend them at their own discretion. States, however, would spend their grants as they do all other revenues for the constantly growing demands of state and local government. To the extent some misuse of funds did occur, it is hard to believe such misuse would lead to worse results than does the budgetary irresponsibility of the present specific grants program.

The Benson-McClelland study notes these advantages in consolidated grants:

Consolidated grants would restore the governor's administrative, as well as fiscal, control of his departments, thus eliminating the problem of governors finding their own subordinate agencies depending on the National Government both for funds and for direction. . . .

The use of consolidated grants should also help the National Government. Even it has found specific grants-in-aid troublesome. These grants have grown without plan; they are carried on by multitudinous bureaus and agencies; they involve duplication of effort; they entail specific consideration of minute and isolated

---

[1] *Consolidated Grants, A Means of Maintaining Fiscal Responsibility* (Washington, D.C.: American Enterprise Association, 1961).

functions, without reference to alternative uses of the resources for the same function through other national grants or for different functions. From a budgetary standpoint the current fragmented approach leaves much to be desired in comparison with consolidated grants, where national expenditures for alternative broad areas of expenditure may be compared.

These alternatives are quite common in the Western countries. The Benson-McClelland study describes their application in various forms in Canada, Australia, and Britain.

The advantage in such general or consolidated grants in getting the Federal bureaucracy out of the affairs of the states is obvious. The effect would also be a considerable reduction in the number of Federal bureaucrats.

An even greater advantage should be to lessen the deplorable influence now enjoyed by pressure groups and lobbies in Washington. Under general or consolidated grants such agencies and lobbies would be compelled to scatter their activities among the capitols of fifty states. This would in a very large degree lessen their insidious power.

CHAPTER 36

Sound Monetary Policy

THE Constitution says that "Congress shall have power ... to coin money, regulate the value thereof." This was to terminate the inflationary practices of the states under the Articles of Confederation. The clear intent to maintain stability was observed during most of the years prior to 1900 by keeping our currency on a bimetallic standard. The value of silver and gold changed from time to time, but in 1873 silver was demonetized and in the Hayes Administration specie payment was resumed. Substantially until 1900, and legally after 1900, gold was the standard of value until 1933, when the gold standard was abandoned.

In international dealing, however, the United States still has been able to convert its currency. Since international financial transactions are a large element in business calculations, ability to convert has advantages in restraining inflation at home. With credit, inflation rises. Attracted by higher prices, foreign goods flow in and exports decline. Our gold supply flows out. This leads to a contraction of bank credit, and thus inflation is measurably restrained. The importance of the character of our currency is underlined in a speech by Gabriel Hauge, economic adviser to President Eisenhower and now a banker in New York:

> Retribution is sure and not slow. For the quality of our currency is a reflection of our national character. A poor credit risk

needs sound collateral. Persistent gold outflows can imply distrust of the dollar, and so a large gold stock is necessary collateral for weak national character. If we do not discipline ourselves at home, if we do not put our domestic affairs in order, we can be quickly brought to heel by other nations. A trustworthy currency is more than a mark of solvency; it is an aspect of national sovereignty.

Since 1933 a considerable body of opinion has advocated the return of gold to domestic convertibility. Its arguments go back to the original principle that the rate of gold production is limited by nature.

If an administration comes to power dedicated to a return to the gold standard the approach must be through preliminary steps. Henry Hazlitt of *Newsweek* has suggested the following as a procedure by such a government dedicated to maintaining a sound and stable currency:

1. The Administration will immediately announce its intention to return to a full gold standard by a series of steps dated in advance. The Federal Reserve Banks and the Treasury will temporarily suspend all sales and purchases of gold, merely holding what they have. Simultaneously with this step, a free market in gold will be permitted.

2. After watching this market, and meanwhile preventing any further inflation, the government, within the period of not more than a year, will announce the dollar-gold ratio (the "price" of gold) at which convertibility will take place.

3. On and after Convertibility Day, and for the following six months, any holder of dollars will be entitled to convert them into gold bars, but at a moderate discount in the paper dollars he turns in. . . .

4. Six months after Convertibility Day, the country will return to a full gold-bullion standard. . . .

5. One year later still, on January 1, 19——, the country will return to a full gold-coin standard, by minting gold coins and permitting free conversion. A full gold-coin standard is desirable because a gold-bullion standard is merely a rich man's standard.

A relatively poor man should be just as able to protect himself against inflation, to the extent of his dollar holdings, as a rich man.[1]

A return to the gold standard, however desirable, cannot in itself provide a complete restraint on inflation. Congress would still have the power to take us off the gold standard. It is neither a mere gadget nor a cure-all. It is, as Hazlitt says, a part of a "sound monetary policy . . . under which governments respect private property, economize in spending, balance their budgets, keep their promises, and refuse to connive in over-expansion of money or credit."

Even an Administration such as that of Eisenhower, with a sincere desire to maintain the integrity of the dollar, was unable to infuse in Congress a sense of fiscal responsibility. As prospects for the next few years become clear, those who favor a return to the gold standard may have to wait. They should, however, keep the issue before the American people as an objective. Meanwhile the hope for sound money rests upon two more immediately attainable ends—strengthening elements in Congress that favor greater economy, and insuring the independence and fiscal soundness of the Federal Reserve System.

Sheer manufacture of money by deficit financing is a major factor in inflation. Another is, and to a degree always has been, an equal threat, the overexpansion of credit. The first depends upon the posture of Congress, while the regulation and measurable control of credit is vested in the Federal Reserve System and its Board of Governors.

The architect of the Federal Reserve Act, passed in 1913, was Carter Glass, chairman of the House Banking and Currency Committee. Assisted by President Wilson, he won his battle with William Jennings Bryan, then Secretary of State, and other soft-money exponents.

[1] Henry Hazlitt, *What You Should Know About Inflation* (Copyright 1960, D. Van Nostrand Company, Inc., Princeton, N. J.), pp. 59, 60.

The act was to provide "Federal Reserve Banks, to furnish an elastic currency, to afford means of rediscounting commercial paper, to establish a more effective supervision of banking in the United States, and for other purposes." The Board of Governors holds great powers. To prevent dangerous credit expansion or contraction it can regulate the requirements for reserves maintained by member banks. It has power to fix margin requirements in open lending on the security of stocks and bonds. It prescribes regulations for consumer and real estate credits. In short, so far as possible, the Board has responsibility to control speculative activities.

Since no President or Congress can be entrusted with the power over credit because of its potential political use, the Board is largely independent. Its seven members are appointed for terms of fourteen years to prevent so far as possible "packing" by Presidential appointments. The ideal is complete independence. The actuality is measurable co-operation between the Board and the Treasury.

In the creation of the Federal Reserve System, Carter Glass depended very heavily upon H. Parker Willis, Professor of Finance at Columbia, who was, in a very real sense, coauthor of the 1913 act. Later, Professor Willis' most brilliant student was Dr. Ralph Robey, who has distinguished himself on the Columbia faculty and as a journalist and consultant on financial affairs. I have asked Dr. Robey to sum up his estimate of how successful the Federal Reserve System is and may be in the vital area of credit control:

1. A majority is of the opinion that the Federal Reserve Board should be independent of political pressures. To accomplish this the original act provided that Federal Reserve Banks pay the expenses of the Board, not Congressional appropriations. But there is little agreement on just what independence means. The present Chairman interprets it to mean "independent within the Administration" and this perhaps is as much as can be hoped for.

2. Even wider disagreement exists that the Federal Reserve System cannot carry the entire load of stable prices, economic growth, or what-have-you. The Federal Government itself through its spending, taxing, and regulatory agencies is enormously important.

3. The Federal Reserve does have the responsibility of providing an adequate supply of money, but no one knows quite what this means. It does not mean a mechanical increase of such-and-such per cent, although there are some advocates of this policy. Theoretically, the money is also materially influenced by the rate of turnover, and no one can forecast with any practical confidence as to how this will change.

4. The system is following a contra-cyclical policy. This means that if, in the Board's judgment, business is increasing too rapidly and there is danger of inflation, the system can place restraint on the lending power of commercial banks. Conversely, if business starts to slide off, the system provides additional lending power. Many persons think this is the wrong policy, that the Federal Reserve should adopt a policy designed to give the nation a long-term growth with relatively stable prices. This difference of opinion may continue for many decades.

5. It is widely felt that the Federal Reserve should do everything that it can to maintain reasonable stability of prices. There is a good bit the Reserve System can do. By providing credit expansion it may assure an inflationary trend. But there is a lot the Federal Reserve cannot do, such as prohibition of wage increases that force higher costs of production and necessitate price increases. When this takes place, if the Federal Reserve does not permit the expansion of credit adequate to take care of these increased costs and higher prices, the inevitable result is increased unemployment and terrific political pressure on the Reserve authorities.

6. The Federal Reserve influence on commercial banks' lending is through the legally required reserves. The Board has the authority to change requirements within specified limits. Through its buying and selling of Government obligations it either adds or subtracts from member bank reserves. Changes in the rediscount rate do not alter the amount of reserve in the member banks, but merely what it costs to rediscount.

7. The system holds only gold certificates. The Federal Reserve has no authority to change the price of gold, and it neither buys nor sells the actual metal.

8. Federal Reserve policy must consistently take into account our relationship with the rest of the world. If our interest rates are low in relation to those of other major financial centers, we get a substantial outflow of funds and much of this may be in the form of gold itself. This has been an especially important factor recently.

William McChesney Martin, Jr., whose capacity and dedication are widely recognized, was appointed Chairman in 1951 and has three more years to serve. Mr. Martin has stated certain principles under which the Board operates.

He points out that, while the system can make an important contribution to improving the people's economic condition, business and employment do not live on credit alone. He recognizes that the framers of the act "took what seem to me some very wise precautions to see that required judgments would be, in so far as human capacities permit, impartial, informed, and in the interests of the country as a whole." When the power of money management was entrusted to the system care was taken to safeguard it from private interests and political interests.

Chairman Martin holds that

the Federal Reserve's operations in the money field must be conducted with recognition of the Government's borrowing requirements through the U. S. Treasury for two reasons: first, the Federal Reserve has a duty to prevent financial panics, and a panic surely would follow if the Government could not pay its bills; second, it would be preposterous for the Federal Reserve to say that it didn't approve of authorized expenditures and wouldn't help enable the Treasury to finance them.

There is a reciprocal obligation of the Treasury to conduct its operations with recognition of the system's responsibilities. It should not expect the Federal Reserve to inflate the money supply "merely so that Treasury could get money at an artificially low rate." So, with complementary responsibilities, the two work together.

Neither can ignore what interest rates should be. Martin points out that "the forces of the market must be allowed to operate, and to be reflected in interest rates, but it would be fantastic for the economy to be stifled by unavailability of credit." For this vast country's regional and seasonal requirements must be met.

Martin recognizes that another factor in considering monetary policy is that of growth. The volume of money must grow with population and "the growing scale of economic activity and productive capacity, so the base of bank reserves must be expanded accordingly. How much growth there should be is more difficult to say. I do not profess to know what the figure ought to be, and I doubt that a precise figure can be set as desirable for year-in-and-year-out purposes." In short, money growth must be related to the country's real needs.

Hence in practice the Federal Reserve System can aid a prudent Administration to restrain inflation, and in a very important way the Federal Reserve Board can measurably restrain a profligate government. But it has not sustained and cannot sustain a sound dollar alone. The value of the 1946 dollar has declined to sixty-five cents. In preceding years the shrinkage was very considerable.

The problem, then, finally comes down to the kind of President and Congress we put in office. Upon the extent to which these instruments of power respond to the imperatives of guarding the value of the nation's money through prudent expenditures must rest the economic welfare of all individuals and the enduring heritage and power of the country.

CHAPTER 37

Tolerable Tax Policies

THERE are certain principles that should apply to all taxation. The first succinct statement in Britain of such principles is in Adam Smith's *Wealth of Nations,* published in 1776. With variations his four maxims have survived the test of time. In a somewhat different arrangement, Henry George stated them a century later in *Progress and Poverty,* measuring them against the virtues of land value taxation. Combining the Smith and the George principles to meet contemporary conditions, the four principles are:

1. A tax should bear as lightly as possible on the production of wealth. It should not decrease the general fund from which taxes must be paid and the community maintained. It should encourage the taking of risk which is embodied in individual initiative, innovation, and the expenditure of individual efforts in profitable labor. Thus, it should always encourage saving and investment in productive enterprise.

2. A tax should be easily and cheaply collected and also bear as directly as possible upon the ultimate payer. It should be clear and understandable. The more that the individual knows he is taxed and feels the burden, the more alert he will be as a citizen in evaluating the spending policies of his government.

3. In the imposition of taxes there should be the least possible

temptation and opportunity for corruption by the tax gatherer and for cheating, dodging, avoidance, and evasion by the taxpayer.

4. A tax should bear equitably so as to give no citizens an advantage or put any citizen at a disadvantage in comparison with others.

I should add as Number 5 a principle that could not have been understood in the eras of Smith and George. In the imposition of Federal taxes the constitutional framework of the nation should be guarded. Many tax sources now used by the Federal government belong by constitutional right to the states and local governments. So far as possible, these sources should be returned, thus reducing considerably Federal grants-in-aid.

Mr. René Wormser,[1] with whom I have discussed the substance of this chapter, suggests certain additional principles of taxation:

1. Taxes should not discriminate against the self-employed.

2. They should not penalize those who have erratic incomes (by demolishing occasional or rare peaks of income in any one year).

3. They must, so far as is practicable, protect the taxpayer against violations of his privacy.

4. They must take account of the fact that if there is a progressive rate system the rates increase automatically by the operation of inflation. The result is a progressive, yearly increase of true rates in relation to purchasing power.

5. They must not confiscate capital. The capital gains tax calls an increase in capital substantially an addition to income, although it may be at a lower rate than the normal income tax.

Even a cursory examination of our Federal tax structure shows that it has violated all of the foregoing general principles. Moreover, the income tax has already gone beyond the limit of its productivity. This means that the present tax structure is an inflationary force.

---

[1] Mr. Wormser is a distinguished tax and estate lawyer whose texts, including *Wormser's Guide to Estate Planning,* are well known among tax experts.

In any tax reform the fifth principle should be stressed. As a means of strengthening the capacity of the states to secure adequate revenue and to cut back the practice of Federal grants-in-aid, certain tax sources should be made available to them. All death and inheritance taxes so far as possible should be collected by the states for their purposes. Mr. Wormser suggests the following as a means to that end:

I agree that estate and inheritance taxation should be confined to the states. However, if we are to adopt the theory that death taxes should be high, as an offset (on a social theory) to lowering top income tax brackets, then there might have to be some Federal integration. This could be accomplished easily if the law were changed so that the Federal rates of estate tax were high but the estate would be entitled to a deduction or offset in full for state death taxes paid. There is a partial credit now, but if it were a credit in full, the states would enact rates sufficient to wipe out the Federal tax through offset and thus take the full tax unto themselves. Any state which did not do so would be crazy.

In further enlarging the capacity of states and local communities to meet their own needs, many excise taxes now so heavily appropriated by the Federal government should be released to the states.

In considering the possible reform of the Federal income tax, I have found the most cogent and reasonable series of suggestions in a small and readable book by Dan Throop Smith of the Harvard School of Business, who served in the United States Treasury for several years during the Eisenhower Administration.[2] The conclusions of the book are summed up in brief "packages" of reform.

In the suggestions which follow I have been considerably influenced by Professor Smith's practical suggestions as well as by the suggestions of Mr. Wormser. I hold neither responsible for my interpretations and variations.

[2] *Federal Tax Reform* (New York: McGraw-Hill, 1961).

There seems to be fairly general agreement that some sort of progression in tax rates is not only inevitable but desirable. The principle of progression, however, has been applied so heavily that it has introduced many undesirable forms of avoidance. The high brackets actually now yield a relatively small amount of revenue.

Many would return to proportional taxation on incomes, a form somewhat like the ancient system of tithes. For example, if the government needs 25 per cent of the national income, then impose a 25 per cent tax on all incomes, large and small.

A capital gains tax is, as its name suggests, a levy on capital. Thus it is vigorously opposed in toto by many economists. But Smith suggests as the most desirable reform tax-free shifts in investments of all kinds, with normal income tax on whatever part of the proceeds is not reinvested. In the present law an individual may sell his residence and escape a capital gains tax if he reinvests in another residence. If this be legitimate for that form of gain, there is no valid reason why it should not apply to all other capital gains.

As is obvious, the 52 per cent tax on corporations is in reality a hidden excise on consumers. It should be reduced progressively year by year, perhaps by 1 per cent a year for a specified number of years.

Political talk is periodically filled with promises to eliminate "loopholes." A favorite topic is tighter restrictions on expense account deductions. This is, within reason, a wise reform and could be achieved by judicious administrative action. The gain in revenues would be small.

A much larger loophole is often attacked but never closed. This is tax-exemption privileges accorded to co-operatives, mutual fire and casualty insurance companies, mutual savings banks, and loan associations. Since many of these favored enterprises compete with tax-burdened businesses, they should be subject to exactly the same tax as their competitors. Merely to tax member beneficiaries would not eliminate the element of unfair competition.[3]

In the foregoing pages of this chapter I have from time to time stressed the need for a pattern of tax changes which will stimulate more private investment—in short, a greater formation of capital funds. This need underlies most of the proposals I have made, especially a reduction of tax rates and also greater deductions for depreciation. It should be added that the need for capital formation is a major reason why inflation is such a deadly threat. For inflation's diet is what was laboriously put away yesterday. Inflation feeds on savings.

The liberal says his concern is for "the little fellow," who he believes can be helped by excessive exactions from the well-to-do and the corporations.

But neither the little fellow nor the big fellow nor the corporation is "an Iland, intire of it selfe." All of us are parts of an integrated economy. An injury which halts the growth of that economy is an injury to all, and that economy is dependent upon savings, capital accumulation, and investment in capital goods. The long-range consequences of insufficient savings and capital formation have now been elaborately documented in one of the most massive undertakings in economic research in modern times. Since 1950, the National Bureau of Economic Research has been engaged in a study of capital formation and financing. Seven volumes in this field have been published. The final one, *Capital in the American Economy*,[4] was written by Simon Kuznets, professor of Economics at Harvard and a staff member of the National Bureau for more than thirty years. After examining the record of a period of eighty-five years, his conclusion is that there

---

[3] A cautious approach to heavier taxes on these institutions is now before Congress.

[4] Princeton, N.J.: Princeton University Press, 1961.

has been an alarming relative decline in net capital formation, especially in recent years. There has been, to be sure, a marked increase in gross savings, even when corrections are made for changes in the value of the dollar. But considering the vastly greater need for capital now and in the years ahead, its relatively slow growth is insufficient.

CONCLUSION

The Moral Imperative of Leadership

THE challenge of our times is to fulfill the moral imperative of responsible leadership of the nation in the world as well as of the individual in the nation. The first cannot be bought. In our world it must accrue from example and persuasion. Realism and strength, courage and optimism, faith and good works, moral and material wealth, knowledge and wisdom—all bear upon its excellence. All are indivisible.

Peoples outside the Communist sphere live in the presence of an armed, aggressive force. Forthright and devious subversion is on every hand. It is for the strong to provide the requisite leadership to defeat Communist purposes. For us this means that our paramount obligation and objective is a long-range, hard-won thing—leadership among nations.

But the first imperative is untenable without the second—individual leadership. Such leadership is a quality which may serve a variety of purposes. It may benefit or it may betray. It may strengthen or it may erode. It may secure and maintain liberty or it may bring on serfdom. It is an attribute given to those who can and will exercise it. Few men are born to it. In life it is acquired, usually by resolve, by training, and to a degree by chance.

There is too much acceptance of a notion, cultivated in cozy, academic studies by men in scratchy tweeds with an aroma of good tobacco, that "progress" stretches before us in the direction

257

of collectivism, centralized authority, leveling, and the elimination of not only needs but wants. The catchwords and involuted paragraphs of this fraternity draw nourishment from European theories of the last century and more recent wishful thinking of British and continental economists and sociologists. Khrushchev's straight talk that "history" is on his side and that Communism is the "wave of the future" is to the point and a relief by comparison. Some of our liberal leaders speculate that the ultimate "answer" in our troubled world will be a "meeting" with Communism somewhere as we "progress" and as Soviet countries "change" and move away from their present extreme position and become more "tolerant." It is just a matter of time, they say.

The conservative alternative, which calls for outstanding individual leadership at all levels of our society, is a positive assertion of the imperatives of individualism and those of our religious ethic. Ministrations from the proliferating jumble of offices spread for miles around the Potomac Basin are eroding what has been our heritage and strength. Must we go to the arid plateau of the superstate to see what we forfeit?

The alternative can be attained only by the efforts of uncommonly good and brave men and women. Unremitting attention and hard work are involved. Perhaps this arduous prospect is what inspires so many comfortable excuses for inaction. One of these is the belief that a Presidential Moses will lead us out of danger. But the election of no single individual to the Presidency could solve the problems that beset us. Even an authentic Moses could not save us single-handed, and there is always the chance that the man elected might not be Moses at all. To those who suffer this delusion I suggest the case of the Frenchman who decided to ignore the French Revolution.

Another excuse is the expression of inadequacy in the face of "trends" and public opinion polls. A number of hard truths should be made clear about these popular phenomena and about public opinion generally.

In the years since 1933, when I began to write about politics for publication, I have traveled a great deal over the states and communities of America. In the course of these adventures in reporting I have never made it a practice to avail myself of the opportunity to talk with people indiscriminately "at the crossroads and byways." Rather, I have found it rewarding to discuss conditions and opinions with reporters, editors, and politicians who themselves have had a hand in shaping public opinion. They are the ones whose innumerable contacts give them a sense of what a generalized public accepts and what it rejects. This, I find, leads to estimates and conclusions which are generally far more accurate than those gained from public opinion polls.

Experienced politicians have a double objective. They must, if they are to survive, not only take a position which may well be acceptable to their constituents but also accurately appraise how far they can go in shaping public acceptance.

While some polls have their uses, I have always had a generous amount of skepticism about public opinion surveys. The perils which such soundings face are in sampling, in the large number of those interviewed who have no opinions at all, the reticence of people in telling what they think or prefer, and the fact that answers given on the spur of the moment are frequently different than those given after full consideration. The shaping of the questions has a great deal to do with predetermining the answers. There is also the partiality of those who "interpret" opinion surveys.

In pursuit of what Edmund Burke called the "phantoms we are and what phantoms we pursue," Professor V. O. Key, Jr. has written a large volume, *Public Opinion and American Democracy*.[1] Although Key's analysis is almost as unintelligible as the studies he examined, there are evidences that he made a valiant effort to penetrate the inscrutable.

Key quite wisely concludes, however, that mass opinion repre-

[1] New York: Alfred A. Knopf, 1961.

sents an "interaction" between what he calls "influentials" and the bulk of the people, who are under the influence of their leaders' "cues," "proposals," and "visions." Those leaders are the political "activists." If the masses are deluded and corrupted, it is because leaders have so willed it. If the best in human nature manifests itself, it is because they have had wise and morally inspired leaders. Thus, the "health of the democratic order" depends upon the beliefs, standards, and competence of leadership.

This conclusion confirms what I have always believed since I came to grips with the realities of politics. Key's estimate of nearly forty years of public opinion research confirms what practical politicians have always known.

It is a gross exaggeration to say that a successful, experienced politician "follows" public opinion. His calculations are so seemingly casual that he appears sometimes to guide himself by instinct alone. By a process of trial and error, mixed by some contacts with individuals in his constituency, he calculates the quality and intensity of the response he will get to certain issues. Then he articulates a rationale and an appeal designed to stir the emotions as well as thought. Thus he largely creates a response from his constituents.

The politician seems to follow public opinion, while he actually leads it. If the politician is activated by a moral concern for the good of his constituents, his calculations include an appraisal of the long-term welfare of the people he seeks to persuade. If he is a mere demagogue, his concern is his immediate personal interests. The demagogue's professed concern for his "people" is mere sham. He is not concerned about long-term consequences. The "visions" he induces are illusions. His "proposals" are usually self-defeating. His "cues" may be incitements to unreasoning passions of greed and hatred.

This is why responsible leadership so greatly involves a moral imperative to serve the long-term as well as the immediate good. The way to satisfy the need for this leadership is through the political participation of those who have the talents, the courage, the opportunity, and the conscience to serve at all levels, from the community to the nation.

Politics is not an austere piece of drudging duty. For it teems with the elements of high adventure. In politics we come to grips with all that is challenging in human life. There is revealed in politics the glamor and the grime of human nature; its fascinating but inscrutable complexities; its narrow alleys and broad highways; its dizzying sense of change. Politics dashes the hopes of the scientist who would measure it and exacts the utmost from the artist who would depict it.

It is not merely a game or a business. In our society it is the delicate process by which free men seek a compromise between freedom and order. Whether we are aware of it or not, politics rests a heavy hand on every circumstance of our lives. It takes our money and spends it. It can tell us how much we can save and what interest we can get. It can measurably determine what job we may have and what we may get for our labor. It can take our children and decree what they shall be taught. It can take our youth and destroy them in war. It can enter our dwellings and seize our private effects. If we go on as we have, it will regiment our lives from conception to dissolution. Even our quiet graves are made to specifications drawn by a bureaucrat.

Certainly politics is not something to avoid or abolish or destroy. It is a condition, like the atmosphere we breathe. It is something to live with, to influence if we wish, and to control if we can. We must master its ways or we shall be mastered by those who do.

The evidence of our incomparable achievement in technology and industrial management is all around us. The institutions of our republic surround us, too. The achievements of Americans are written on the luminous pages of history. These are the products of a hardy race enjoying the bracing climate of a classless society. They are the creations of free men and women dedicated to the ideal of liberty.

Our nation has achieved miracles of productivity, of efficiency, and inventive genius. Its abundance is far beyond our needs.

But all this may pass if we neglect our basic political institutions. Busy with the material things we are creating, we forget the preservation of those values which give meaning and purpose to life and which in the long run determine material progress. The political institutions we have inherited seem to us so excellent that we foolishly assume that they need no attention and support. In enjoying the excellence of the fruit we are blind to the care of the tree.

This incomparable land of ours was, it is true, blessed by nature with protective oceans and with superabundant resources. But these alone do not make a civilization. That is built by human beings, in our case by imaginative, venturesome, creative, and hard-working individuals dedicated to liberty. They came from many older nations. They held high the ideals of a classless society, government by the consent of all, with political parties to channel opinion into national policy. This civilization and its political institutions are ours to cherish in mastery or meanly, bitterly to lose.

> "Knowledge we ask not. Knowledge thou hast lent.
> The will to do, there lies the bitter need.
> Give us to build above the deep intent,
> The deed, the deed!"

Index